SEED TO VASE

ROZ CHANDLER

CONTENTS

DEDICATION

To my beautiful family, my husband Andrew for always inspiring me to follow my dreams and my two children Emily and Holly for encouraging me to just do it. No flower blooms without love. I am forever grateful for their support.

INTRODUCTION

Why Flowers?

Even after a decade of growing and arranging, I still get incredible joy from flowers and from sharing flowers. Even when it's pouring down with rain, or the ground is frozen solid, there's nothing I love more than what I do – and I feel so lucky.

I also feel incredibly blessed to share this joy with men and women across the globe. Throughout my time in the flower industry, I've seen flowers transform lives and health; help people to manage the stresses and strains of life, to overcome bereavement, ill health and help them to cope with mental health issues, help them to find a way out of impossible situations and into a new life.

When I am up to my elbows in soil, focusing on pricking out or planting seeds or tubers my brain is fully focused – I can't think about accounts or the weekly shop – and it's just amazing!

The Royal Horticultural Society (RHS) has done some in-depth research into how gardens and gardening can make us feel better, how growing is actually magic and how, "The act of gardening helps us to keep fit and connect with others, to enjoy and be part of nature and to revel in colour, aroma, wildlife and beauty."

"Simply contemplating nature helps to rest and recharge our brains," wrote Professor Alistair Griffiths for the RHS – a truer phrase has never been spoken.

Throughout this book you will read incredible stories of people from across the country who have used growing flowers to help them overcome extraordinary situations; from losing a daughter to recovering from executive burnout – the transformative power of nature is immense and something I will never stop shouting about.

From Seed to Vase

I had been running my flower farm for nearly ten years when the pandemic hit the UK in the spring of 2020. This threw a spanner in the works! With weddings off the agenda for who-knew-how-long, and a field of beautiful seasonal blooms all ready to be cut and conditioned, I, like so many entrepreneurs had to get creative- but what to do?

So, in the middle of the Covid-19 pandemic, I set about putting an online course together to help people to grow their own British cut flowers, subsequently launching The Seed to Vase course.

As my journey began, I was joined by almost 200 others from right across the UK and beyond; from the north of Scotland to the Channel Islands and everywhere in between. From Scottish castles to apartment blocks in London, I was truly amazed by the response to the course.

People took this journey for so many different reasons, and I salute them all. In this book are their individual journeys which I hope you will enjoy reading. Some were bereaved and found comfort in nature, others just needed to achieve something. Some wanted to grow blooms as a business and others joined purely for fun. What united us all was the desire to grow our own flowers for cutting in our gardens, learn about seed germination, pests and diseases, composting, annuals, biennials, perennials and so much more.

Online masterclasses were held covering the finer points of growing and caring for Roses, Dahlias, Sweet Peas and Peonies, as well as composting across the 70 training sessions.

This year I have been humbled by the support I have received. I often get letters in the post saying how the Seed to Vase course has changed lives and that I am seen as someone who inspires and has bundles of energy – how lovely is that?

The course and our work have also received some incredible press attention. Field Gate Flowers featured in the *Mail On Sunday, Female First, Vogue and Homes and Gardens*. I have met some truly inspirational people online and connected via social media channels too so many others. For me 2020/2021, although a year of global destruction and great sadness, has been one of reflection and fuelling a new determination to change things.

The Coronavirus pandemic, although harrowing and debilitating in ways we cannot imagine, has allowed us to stop, breathe and spend time outdoors. I have seen a wave of people looking to grow their own vegetables or flowers, moving the view that growing is for the older generation, those with disposable income and time. Now, the images of Volvo cars and elderly couples in garden centres are a thing of the past (don't get me wrong I am not against this but it's lovely to see all generations taking to gardening) and Instagram is flooded with a new generation of growers. I for one am delighted to see everyone getting involved and, taking it back to my passion – the more people that grow their own flowers, the more we will reduce imports into the UK, and I really hope that the Seed to Vase course is the first step of a legacy that changes the way we view British flowers in the future.

All that said, this book isn't about me – it's about everyone who came together in a time of a global pandemic with the minds open for learning – I salute each one of you who put their faith in me and joined me on the journey. Receiving lovely words each week on email, on cards in the posts – little notes of thanks and messages on how we have changed people's lives has been truly humbling. Thank you.

So, where did it all begin?

I am Roz Chandler, a British flower farmer and florist based just outside Milton Keynes.

I can already hear you saying 'Milton Keynes? Isn't that the home of the concrete cows? It's not known for its areas of parkland and open green spaces.'

Well, if you are saying that you'd be wrong! Milton Keynes is full of parkland and is, in fact, a very green city with a very busy Parks Trust. (Sorry - I can get very defensive of the beautiful city I call home when people mention concrete cows and roundabouts).

Anyway, I was fortunate enough to be able to buy a rather run-down house with five acres of land in a small village to the north of Milton Keynes in 2007. This is the place that my husband Andrew and I, along with our two children (then just about to become teenagers), still call home. They do say patience is a virtue, but by the time we found our beautiful home, mine was running out.

I have always been a firm believer that land should be used and not wasted. I'm also a keen researcher and learner. For me, learning is something you do through your whole life, and I believe every day is a school day. Today, for instance, I learned of someone in a London flat growing Dahlia in dustbins – now who would have thought you could do that?

My day job involves writing course material, researching content, finding guest speakers that I feel will add something to our courses, managing all our social media channels, weeding, watering, propagating, meeting brides and grooms to talk about their special days, cutting and conditioning blooms for bouquets and DIY buckets - there certainly couldn't be a more varied job and I truly love it.

Before sitting at my computer today I've been assuming the role of a structural engineer, working out what structure and trussing we need to cover a 324sqm marquee roof... I am a writer, researcher, gardener, marketeer, photographer, salesperson, project manager, finance manager, negotiator and now structural engineer, who knows enough about weight-bearing loads of branches and trees.

How did it all start?

Let me take you back to 1963 - the year I was born. My parents - both hard-working individuals - always dreamed of owning their own home. By the late 1970s, they'd managed to purchase their first three-bedroom house in the new town of Hemel Hempstead - and they had worked hard to get to that point.

Gardening isn't something I have strong childhood memories of - I certainly didn't come from a family of gardeners; motivated hard workers that followed their dreams, yes - but not gardeners. Neither of my parents were florists so I can honestly say I had no prior knowledge of how to arrange – and I didn't have a childhood that saw me spending summers with my grandparents, playing and learning all about nature. Sorry, that just wasn't me.

That said, I can pinpoint a few things that went on in my childhood that, in hindsight, did send me in the direction of my future.

I remember being a child that loved being outdoors, making perfume from the red roses that adorned the fronts of all the gardens in my street. I also remember going to France as an exchange student at the age of 13 and spending a glorious month in the southwest of the country with my pen pal's family at their farm in a remote village. Her father was the Mairie (Mayor) and worked the land.

I can't remember another time in my life that I felt so carefree and happy – cycling along the lanes, making daisy chains and spending time on the land.

A few years later, I met someone who was looking into agricultural courses, this sounded okay, so in true Roz fashion, I jumped straight in and applied for a degree course that I had no knowledge of but sounded fun. I found myself on a course that would lead to a BSC (Hons) in Environmental Science. In truth, I think I fancied all the outdoor field trips (putting the mention of visiting coal mines in South Wales to the back of my mind) and I found myself driving my 850cc Mini down the M4 (the M25 wasn't even completed at this time - that shows you how old I am).

Three years later and, with a degree under my belt, I had learned all about sustainability, pollution, and the environment. Indeed, I felt quite radical writing my dissertation on the nitrate pollution in the rivers of the United Kingdom from farming and the connection with cancer. Honestly, I felt a true rebel as I crept into the River Lee in Hertfordshire to take samples that then duly took the journey back to Plymouth with me in my trusty Mini.

This was the start of my concern for the environment and a passion to make a change that has been growing ever since.

Fast forward to 2011 and the birth of Field Gate Flowers. In between, there were years on a Greek island, many years working in the events industry and then latterly running my own digital agency and working as an interim Marketing Director. For years I ran the farm and worked, advising all flourishing would-be flower farmers to do the same unless they were prepared for the drop in income that comes with developing a flower business – it's not the easiest way to make an income, but it's certainly the best!

I once read that the happiest people are those who work as florists and gardeners - put them together as a flower farmer, and you certainly have something truly amazing.

Flowers grown by your local flower farmer will be freshly picked and locally delivered, saving thousands of travel miles. Your local flower farmer grows with the seasons and is motivated not by predictable, year-round crops, but by seasonal flowers with the perfume and natural, informal beauty that can only come from small-scale, local production.

Growing your own is even better, and I hope that you will be inspired by the stories in this book too.

 "So, perhaps the best thing to do is to stop writing introductions and get on with the book."

— *AA MILNE*

1

LIFE ON A FLOWER FARM

So, what does life on a flower farm look like? Honestly? It's not beautiful... I mean, of course, it is because there are countless flowers, but there are also lots of weeds, piles of compost and tractors - it's a working farm, just like any other agricultural farm. Sorry to those of you who had a vision of pretty girls wearing gingham dresses with wicker baskets, skipping through the fields. If you did this at Field Gate, you would be stung by nettles and have chunks taken out of you by the odd horsefly.

Across our five-acre plot, we have around three acres that are used for growing. Across those three acres, we have three poly-tunnels – our largest being 125sqm, and two smaller ones, along with ten raised beds and a greenhouse. The growing area is divided into four areas, which my team and I have affection-ally named.

There's 'The Goat Bed', which is the oldest part of the flower farm and one that is nearest to Luna and Ginny our pair of Boar Goats, then there's 'The New Bed', which was built in 2020 to expand our operation. This growing space houses Dahlias and Chrysanthemums, so sometimes we call it the 'Dahlia Bed'.

The Cottage Garden, the area with two polytunnels and raised beds is a sheltered area where our polytunnels house some of our David Austin roses, all of our seedlings at the beginning of any year along with our Chrysanthemums and Zinnias (to extend our growing season). The last of our four growing areas is 'The Allotment' - an area that used to be an allotment (hence the name) and now is home to our annuals.

Each year, we grow around thirty different annuals (hardy and half-hardy) from Ammi to Amaranthus, Cleome to Cornflowers and Sweet Peas to Scabious. We also grow an enormous number of herbs – including seven different types of mint, sage, borage and rosemary.

Our biennials are headed up by the wonderful Sweet William – a firm favourite of ours because of its many different colours and the fact that it is also a very productive grower. More recently, we have added in Foxgloves, Honesty Sweet Rocket as well as wallflowers.

Our favourite perennials here at Field Gate Flowers are Achil-lea, Campanula, Astrantia, Delphiniums, Verbascum, Peonies,

Roses, and Chrysanthemums. We also grow a huge amount of foliage (I always say you can never grow enough) including Eucalyptus, Common Nime Bark, Hornbeam, Euonymus, Pittosporum, Physocapus, Philadelphus, Skimmia, Myrtle (made even more popular after the Royal weddings), Viburnum Tinus and Euphorbias. And then there are the bulbs and tubers – in 2021 we grew 37 varieties in total.

I amazed myself with the varieties of British flowers we grow - and at a rough count, I think that we've reached a huge 100 different blooms and foliage.

Of course, you don't need all these seeds, bulbs and tubers to start a cutting patch. I started with three 3m x 1m raised beds and the rest, as they say, is history.

And of course, I couldn't do all of this without a team – and I am so lucky to be surrounded by the team that I have.

There are the wonderful lads from the village – Elliott and Rob. One is off to Cardiff University to read Mathematics and the other is in year twelve. But without them watering and weeding would be particularly hard.

Emma – my guide on all things propagating and growing is a true friend, and we have grown this business together. Her knowledge is second to none, and those who take one of our courses can vouch for this as they learn all about everything from composting and to nature in the garden.

Sally has just joined us as part of the WRAG scheme, which is wonderful. The WRAG scheme, for those who may not know, was launched in 1993. The full wording for WRAGS is Work and Retrain as a Gardener Scheme and it is run and administered by the WFGA who make it their mission to enhance horticulture.

Floristry is headed up by Clare and Lucie, who could make a brown paper bag look good. I am constantly in awe of their incredible talent.

As I write this, we have added some new team members to our merry crew, Sarah, Steve, Luke and Cheryl. I thank each and everyone of them for the part they play in this wonderful adventure.

And me? Where do I fit in? Well, as you have probably gathered, I fit in just about anywhere! I am the driver, the businesswoman, the podcaster, the writer, the weeder, the waterer, the one who knows what we should grow for who and who to sell it to – an allrounder. In any one day, I can be propagating, cutting, conditioning, arranging, and delivering, hosting a podcast, writing course content, making sure that our social channels are buzzing and keeping it all together – there's not a single dull moment for sure! And to those of you who were part of the 2021 course cohort – yes, I do sleep, but my mission is to truly make a difference to the UK cut flower industry.

I don't apologise for being passionate about this topic. The more we grow, the less we depend on imports from overseas. As a person conscious of air miles, sustainability, and the impact that flying flowers across the world has on the environment – logic dictates to me that if more people could grow their own blooms in their gardens, learn to arrange them and provide them to friends and family – there would be less of a reliance on the plastic-wrapped supermarket imported blooms – and it would reduce the carbon emissions produced by flowers by millions of tons a year. This passion, combined with the belief and knowledge the joy of growing blooms is good for the soul and mental health is what I love most about what I do, and I enjoy nothing more than sharing it.

2

UK FLOWER FARMING

Let's talk British flowers

I remember going to a speaker session a few years back. It was all about your legacy and what you would want people to say at your funeral. Well firstly, before we get on to words, the flowers had better be good – no garage blooms for me thank you very much! Secondly, I would want everyone to say that I was a totally committed and passionate person who made a difference in people's lives, helping our environment and while inspiring others in the industry.

Field Gate Flowers is built on strong foundations which we absolutely do not compromise on. We grow everything without herbicides and pesticides, working with nature and encouraging bees and insects. We grow everything we use to create our displays here in the UK, reducing air miles and providing local employment.

I am passionate about seasonal, British grown and cut flowers. Having flowers flown in from all around the world is unneces-

sary – it's bad for the planet and it does nothing to improve and sustain UK biodiversity

Some facts about the UK flower industry

The cut-flower market in the UK is worth more than £2 billion. With more than 7000 florists in the industry, it may surprise you to know that a huge 90% of the UK's flowers are imported, with the global industry worth more than $55 billion. The majority of the blooms you will see on sale today in your local supermarket, florist, or anywhere else come from as far away as Kenya, Ethiopia, and Columbia. The common perception is that most of our flowers come from Holland, but Holland is in fact the wholesaler for all of Europe thanks to the fact that the Dutch government invested heavily in the 1970s to create the Dutch flower markets.

One key difference you'll notice between seasonally-grown UK flowers and imported blooms is the fact that the imported flowers have very little scent – something we consumers have allowed to grow due to incessant demand for perfect blooms at any time of year – straight-stemmed red roses for Valentine's Day just isn't 'natural'.

There is no legal or statutory requirement for flowers to be labelled, which means that as consumers, we have no knowledge of the provenance of these blooms, thus we can't make an environmentally ethical choice when it comes to purchasing them. Those sunflowers on the garage front? They could be from anywhere in the world. Chances are they aren't from the UK – but if you want them before the season starts, how else can the market meet demand?

Of course, as with any mass market in developing nations, there are reports of questionable practices. Some parts of the industry have been linked to poor conditions for workers and the communities in which they are based. Workers are low-paid, working in an unregulated industry where health risks such as infertility and miscarriage caused by exposure to chemicals are commonplace. Sexual harassment and discrimination are also frequently reported, and as for maternity rights and childcare - well they are non-existent. Communities find themselves deprived of water supplies, which are diverted to meet the needs of the flower growers and the big businesses that operate them – now you know that, can you look at supermarket flowers in the same way again? They don't seem quite so beautiful now, do they?

There's also the huge environmental pressure of mass flower growing, and as pressure grows to address the global climate emergency, a sustainable flower industry – one that endures by positively contributing to people and the planet – has never been more important.

With its high carbon footprint, mass chemical use to increase production and prolong life, and the destruction of habitats and biodiversity, the flower industry is also hugely guilty of generating mass amounts of plastic waste and, in areas of concentrated growth, regularly contaminate land and water.

For our planet, we need to make this change – and it's a small change we can make easily, and relatively cheaply, whether you live on a 100-acre farm or in an apartment block in central London.

I am utterly determined to spread the word of growing seasonal UK flowers and to see every home in the UK with at least a small cut-flower patch, or a window box, or some pots – whatever works in your space. Growing flowers is possible anywhere – it really is.

The UK flower industry needs rapid change too – we need to be encouraging florists to buy British flowers, we need to drop the notion that all bouquets and displays need to be perfectly manicured and that we 'must' have red roses here in February. We need, to get real!

All of this said, it's not all bleak - I have seen some signs of change. I know people are asking more about where their flowers and foliage come from and how they are grown. I am hoping that this demand will fuel the British flower industry, laying the ground for more flower farmers, ethical consumers, and hobby growers – it just needs to go faster.

Why grow British flowers instead of choosing shop-bought flowers?

- Buying British helps the environment by reducing the amount you purchase from overseas.
- By buying flowers grown here in the UK you can support wildlife and the eco-system.
- British flowers grown naturally smell incredible.
- You can grow whatever flowers you like – and you can grow varieties that you can't in the shops such as Sweet Peas, Nigella and Scabious.
- Growing your own keeps you fit and it's incredibly good for mental health and well-being.
- The cost of shop-bought flowers has rocketed- growing your own will save you money in the long-run.
- Every day is a learning day – getting into flower growing will help you to develop so many new skills.

If you do need to buy flowers, here's why you should buy British.

- The flowers will last longer than imported flowers which, by the time they've arrived with you, will have already been cut for a few days.

- British flowers need fewer chemicals to last because they're fresher when you buy them.
- British-grown flowers can be delicate varieties such as poppies, which need to travel in water. Because they have less distance to travel the growers will put their precious little people in buckets of water and deliver like that. Minimum distance means maximum vase life.
- Buying British means that your flowers have a lower carbon footprint due to the short distance they've travelled. We have lots of brides come to us because they love the flowers we grow, and because they don't want their wedding flowers to cost the earth – literally, not financially.
- British-grown flowers are excellent value for money. When they are at their seasonal high, quality goes up and the price comes down.

3

10 TIPS TO HAVING YOUR OWN CUTTING PATCH

> "Well, y'see, we keep looking for home, but we keep finding this pit, so I just thought that if we looked for this pit, we might find home."
>
> — WINNIE THE POOH

The Cutting Patch

You have probably gathered by now how passionate I am about growing, harvesting, and arranging seasonally grown British blooms. I have heard a multitude of different reasons why someone has wanted to start their own cut flower patch – and you'll read some of those as we move through this book, but, in the words of Julie Andrews, 'Let's start at the very beginning.'.

The question I am asked more often than anything else is, 'where do I start?', so I have compiled my top ten tips to get you started.

1) Size doesn't matter

Starting out, you'll will need surprisingly little space for your cutting patch. It is not a garden; it is a patch dedicated to cutting – something totally different. It is an area that you won't mind having bare patches when you pluck blooms from it.

A great size to start with is a raised bed of around 9 metres squared. If you can spare this size, you'll have ample space for fifteen sweet peas, 5 cosmos, 5 dahlias, 5 sunflowers, a row of magnificent cornflowers, along with some roses and a handful of herbs such as mint and rosemary. If you have a little patch, be it a corner of an allotment or somewhere else, you can plan your cutting patch. If you have more space, then you can grow more varieties – think of it in lots of 3m x 3m, but remember, it doesn't have to be a square – a long patch is equally as useful.

2) You don't need to speak Latin to do this!

Wrapping your head around what's an annual, perennial, or biennial will take some time – but please do not worry. There's a lot of jargon used in flower growing, but you don't need to know it all! Here is a quick guide:

Annuals are plants that grow for one season and that is their life span. They are the most abundant crop and give instant satisfaction. At Field Gate 50-60% of our blooms are annuals.

Perennials are plants like delphiniums that come back every year.

Biennials are just that – they pop up every other year.

You grow perennials for reliability, shrubs for foliage, bulbs for early spring colour BUT you grow annuals for delight and sheer abundance.

3) Grow what you love

Above everything, it's important to grow what you love. Grow flowers that remind you of your childhood, when you spent endless days outdoors. Grow the flowers that you had in your wedding bouquet or grow the flowers you fell in love with through poetry or literature.

Some of my favourites are below but you will find lots more in the Garden Dairy chapter.

Ammi Majus: these laced capped white flowers are delicate and beautiful in any arrangement

Cornflowers: traditionally a mix of blues and whites, cultivated varieties come in blues, reds, whites, pinks, and almost black (Black Ball).

Nigella: no cutting patch is complete without Nigella – it's just so beautiful and natural.

Scabious: annual scabious is quick to germinate and easy to grow.

Sweet Peas: known for their beautiful fragrance, these are easy to grow and come in hundreds of varieties.

Dahlias: a must in every garden and there are just so many to choose from.

Amaranthus: A stunning addition to any vase – they come in shades of greens and burgundy.

Cosmos: known as the easiest cut flower to grow, Cosmos is prolific and comes in many colours bringing shape to any vase or arrangement.

Tulips: Here are Field Gate Flowers, we grow up to forty different varieties of Tulips – the range of colours they grow in is just spectacular.

Adding some perennials to your borders to supplement your flower garden is also a good idea - you won't go far wrong if you add Salvias, Lavender, Peonies, Verbena, and Veronicas.

4) Choose your position

Initially, I would recommend somewhere sheltered - the wind is a cut flower gardener's enemy. Building a wall is no use either as the wind will hit it, crash down, and flatten all but the hardiest of plants. Think about using trellis or hedging instead. Even better, use some foliage plants such as Eucalyptus, Viburnum, and Pittosporum as windbreakers and you will be rewarded with endless foliage for your arrangements.

5) Rabbits aren't always cute

At Field Gate, we suffer from intruding rabbits that have a taste for flowers. Don't get me wrong, we love rabbits, but I am known to turn into Mr McGregor when Peter is munching at my Dahlias. For a small plot, think about edging with chicken wire but ensure that the bottom edge is placed beneath the ground.

6) Keep things turning round

Plants are rotated to avoid the build-up of pests and diseases. This isn't such a worry if you are growing all annuals, but once you have the bug and get into a bigger plot rotating your growing space will be essential.

7) Make sure you have some support

Now, this is more important than anything! At Field Gate Flowers we use Heras fencing (yes Mr Chandler owns a construction company, and all sorts of supports are found in the yard), but when you're planting on a smaller scale you will need pea netting, string, and twine, and plenty of canes. Top tip – get the support in for your plants before you think you need to.

8) Get down and dirty

It is always a good idea to know what soil you are dealing with, so it's worth investing in a simple PH and moisture meter from eBay or a local garden centre - it will set you back less than £5. Remember whatever soil you have you will need to add compost and nutrition to it. Annual plants grow from seed to cutting plant in 12 weeks and this takes a lot from the soil which needs to be replaced. Keep a space in your garden for compost - it is the best source of food for your garden.

9) Look after your plant babies

Initially, you may not have the luxury of a greenhouse or poly-tunnel, but don't let that put you off. A good warm windowsill will be a good start – as will a small cold frame. It is always better to start small and build - going big right from the start will be incredibly daunting.

10) An heir and a spare!

A lot of seeds are sown directly into the soil – taking things from seed to plant it takes around 12 weeks, so think about continually sowing and growing. Cornflowers, for instance, are sown every two weeks here, right through the season from April to early July.

But, above all else – have fun and enjoy every minute!

4

ALICE HARE

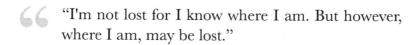 "I'm not lost for I know where I am. But however, where I am, may be lost."

I believe that in life, we all have a journey; a path that we are meant to take. For most of us, we don't manage to get on that path straight away for whatever reason - perhaps the lure of the corporate world, earning the big bucks, family – whatever it is, but I do believe, and I have experienced in my own journey, that whatever path you're intended to be on, you will get there when it's your time.

One of my wonderful course clients, the fabulous Alice Hare, is a perfect example of this.

As a child, Alice was "bathed" in nature, thanks to her father who, in her own words, "Has an amazing amount of knowl-edge about the natural world." – a wealth of knowledge which has passed to her and won her many pieces of cheese on a Trivial Pursuit board over the years!

A busy career woman, with two daughters under 10, two dogs, and a husband, the career path Alice's life followed was one set out for so many women her age, "Making millions for billionaires.".

Overseeing almost 400 pharmacies across England and Wales with a total of 2000 staff, a few years ago Alice started watching Gardener's World. It gave her some respite, an hour of peace at the end of the week in her busy life and, unknowingly, it started to lead her to the road that she finds herself on now.

"I've always enjoyed doing bits in the garden," said Alice. "So, I started planting and growing and it became a weekend hobby. I loved it and found it helped me to relax."

Her garden is known locally as 'The Secret Garden'. Tucked away behind the walls of the town, her initial interest in the cut flower course came from a desire to grow her own wedding flowers. One thing led to another (as it so often does when someone gets the gardening bug) and eventually Instagram led Alice to book a place on my cut flower course – and it was here she really began to find herself.

After joining the Facebook group, she found herself absorbing as much information as she could through the forum, tutorials, and recommended reading as she sat in "dreary hotel rooms" night after night in the name of her job. As part of the community, she learned and developed as her confidence in her creativity and abilities grew. With her own raised beds installed in the garden, she began to see the joy growing your own cut flower garden can bring, and the benefits it can have to mental health.

"Having such a high-pressure job particularly during the pandemic, where I was just sat down on Zoom calls all day was difficult. Between calls, I used to escape to the garden - I'd just go and stand outside and look at the plants and flowers and take in the fresh air- I found it really helped. I just found it so therapeutic"

And then she hit a wall.

After the busiest year of her career, Alice suffered from the plague that's moving through many women in their 40s and 50s – she burned out. She needed a break.

"I was at the railway station in Cardiff. I needed to board the train to Swansea, and I just couldn't do it. I needed to go home and have some time," Alice told me.

"I just needed to stop."

A period of convalescence in the garden followed, and it was here while watching the bees play and seeing life and nature do their thing, Alice's mind began to open and take her to the path that perhaps she'd always been meant to be on. This, compounded with the burnout she was suffering led her to understand that she needed to step away from the rat race and think again.

"The week I crashed, I sat in the garden on the sofa and just looked at everything that I'd spent the last six months creating; everything that I had produced from your course was the therapy I got that week."

"Watching the bees playing and dipping in and out of the Hollyhocks was magical. In fact, I think I spent a whole day doing that!"

Thankfully Alice began to get better quite quickly and was able to turn her attention to her new journey – the journey she'd probably always been meant to be on – a life with nature, growing flowers and offering joy.

"A friend of mine describes this as my period of rewilding," Alice continued.

"I think she's probably right -I've had to completely rewire my thinking."

"My husband is a great believer in happiness being more important than money, whereas I've always worked in the corporate world which is all about making money and big numbers – and this path isn't about that."

As she continues to get well, plans for Alice's own flower farming and floristry business are well underway. With an allotment and 10 beds already in the offing, Alice's journey is now truly heading in the direction she's always been meant to be on – and I am overjoyed!

"I have never been clearer about what I want to do and where I go," Alice enthused as we chatted.

Following her journey, as I did with all the cut flower crew, it was exciting to see her confidence and self-belief grow. In May she told me: "this month I've started telling people that I'm going to be a flower farmer - it's scary saying it to be honest but it's led to so many amazing conversations."

"I'm excited to see what the future holds but I am aware that I want to give back."

As well as working towards creating a sustainable flower farming business that caters for weddings, events and funerals and those special occasional bouquets, Alice is incredibly aware of the therapy that her blooms brought her when she was unwell and she's keen to share that – and with years of pharmaceutical experience and a strong belief in social prescribing, she's perfectly placed to bring that to life.

"I'd love to create somewhere people can come and just be."

"I know that there are lots of people who have been in the same situation as me who aren't lucky enough to have a garden or an outdoor space where they can immerse themselves in nature - I'd love to be able to allow people to just come and sit and watch the bees – as I did."

"I think there's a lot to be said for social prescribing and I would love to take more of a look at how flowers and floristry work within that context."

"I don't know whether it's the floristry, the growing or just being outside that works, but something does, and I'd love to be able to help people that really need it."

"I'd want to be able to invite people to come and play with the flowers – I'd love to be able to give back in that way."

I am excited to see how Alice's business and journey progress. There is so much in her story that resonates with me, and my own journey and I am so glad that sharing my knowledge and my own path can help change lives in this way.

Since we started offering the courses and growing the communities, I am often humbled by people's stories. Many people find the courses and experience of growing flowers for their own enjoyment, and the pleasure of others, to be therapeutic and that's something I am so proud of.

Like Alice, I am never happier or more content than when I am amongst the flowers and nature and am a great believer in the vast mental health benefits nature provides. I can't wait to see where Alice's 'rewilding' takes her.

5

ALISON CUTLAND

 "But the most important thing is, even if we're apart, I'll always be with you."

— A.A. MILNE

A little over two years ago, Alison Cutland received the news that no parent would ever want to hear. Her darling daughter had died in highly unusual circumstances whilst on an internship in Madagascar as part of her degree at Cambridge.

Having passed away in a way that couldn't possibly have been foreseen, the loss felt by her family was monumental – and still is.

Alison and I were talking via Zoom. She was in her car outside a hotel having delivered a training session for work, I was on the farm (as per).

Her strength and tenacity amazed me. As a mother myself, I cannot imagine the grief and heartbreak she has felt, but here she is, taking each day as it comes – and growing beautiful flowers while she's at it.

"Life still seems difficult," she tells me. "But every so often I take a breath and look at how far I have come in the last two years."

The admiration I have for Alison is huge – I think she's amazing. To keep going through the loss of a child and to have come as far as she has is just incredible.

"I've learned to be kind to myself, to take time for myself, and, as small as it is, I'm proud to say that've managed to get out of bed each day."

"There were times when I thought I couldn't carry on, but every day I woke up, my heart beating and so I had to carry on for myself, for my husband, for my son, and for Alana."

With her youngest child having flown the nest for university, the last two years has seen Alison completely throw herself into charity work (more of that to come) and growing her own cut flowers.

"I have always quite liked gardening. I'm not a huge gardener, but I have always loved flowers."

After following the journey of a YouTuber who had acquired some land and decided to use it to grow cut flowers, Alison started her own lockdown growing journey, growing Dahlias and Cosmos and others from seed. The growing bug had truly bitten!

"I got to the point where I wanted more space but moving to a new house is not an option, so I applied for an allotment."

The lease on her own allotment space was signed in January, which coincided with her coming across an advertisement for the Cut Flower Collective.

"I decided that if I was going to grow, I was going to do it properly, so I signed up."

Alison joined the Seed to Vase course as part of the 2021 intake, immersing herself in the community and her growing journey fully.

"I have picked up so many tips along the way – the whole experience has given me a real sense of joy."

"Sometimes, I just sit back and say to myself 'look at what I've achieved' – I am just so proud." As she should be!

The pictures of Alison's allotment are just breath-taking - she's created something so incredibly beautiful.

"The other day I sat down, and I listed all the things I have grown this year, and I thought crikey that's loads."

"I have grown so many things as part of the Cut Flower Collective that I wouldn't have even thought to try before: Cornflowers, Zinnia and so many others – and I love that I've learned things about roses – I've always wanted to grow long stem roses, and I've learned all about that. It's been amazing!"

For Alison, gardening has been a vital tool in helping her to work through her grief and manage her mental health. Like me, she uses it as an anti-dote if she's feeling anxious or

fed up, by allowing herself to get lost in something that absorbs her entire concentration.

"Most people hate weeding, but I just love it," she told me. "You have to really think about what you're doing to make sure you only pull up the weeds. A good stint of weeding allows me to completely zone out – it's so rewarding and is wonderfully mindful."

"Growing has really helped me over the last 18 months. It's brought me so much happiness and peace, and I am so grateful for it."

It is well documented that gardening is good for mental health. Studies have shown how it can help alleviate the symptoms of dementia, reduce stress, boost confidence and self-esteem amongst a whole host of other benefits. I have seen this first-hand so many times, and in Alison, I can see how it's helped her too.

"You don't notice with your own mental health just how you improve day to day, but when you look back over a long period of time you can see how much you've come along."

"I can cope with things I couldn't before, and I think growing has helped that."

I started this chapter with a quote about life and rebirth; for me growing gives me hope - everything comes back around again, and seeing new life each spring gives me such optimism.

"Yes – the same stands for me," Alison agrees. "Planting things, nurturing them, growing beautiful flowers – every bloom is a reward."

"This year I've grown the most gorgeous orange dahlias, which I just love, and I find that while I'm nurturing my flowers, I'm not thinking about all of the things that have happened over the last two-and-a-half years."

It's not only on her allotment and in her garden that she has been growing hope. In the wake of Alana's passing, Alison and her husband threw themselves into setting up a charity in their daughter's name, with the aim of leaving a legacy that will help others.

The Alana Cutland bursary was set up by Alison and Neil with two key aims: the first is to rebuild a school in Madagascar as a way of saying thank you for their support in wake of their daughter's passing. The second aim is to raise money to help women studying at Cambridge receive the support they need to work on projects that do good across the world.

With an initial goal of £5000, at the time of writing, the bursary has raised more than £35,000 and shows no sign of slowing down.

"Alana was passionate about women and their roles in society and how, at school, they outperform boys yet when they get into the workplace, they're on the back foot, struggling to earn as much as their male counterparts as they progress through their careers."

"We'd have really animated conversations about it – she was so well informed and really cared about equality and fairness. So, we decided that part of her legacy should be a fund that finances girls that study at Cambridge to go off and do projects to help others."

The other purpose of the fund will help rebuild a school in Madagascar. As one of the world's most poverty-stricken countries, the gift of education is invaluable and will make such a difference to lives there. Like Alison, I agree that the best route out of poverty is education and share the same hope as her – that this legacy will change lives.

"I am proud to say that the Alana Cutland project has helped so many people – it's a wonderful legacy."

Alison's story has touched me deeply. To know that she has found such solace in growing is something so incredibly special – I am so glad she signed up to join us, and so, so glad it's helped her through this incredibly tough period.

"The grief is always there; it never goes away," she continues. "But gardening – it helps me reset my stress levels, gives me direction and purpose, and helps me to cope."

"I stand at my plot and think 'wow' – it's made a big difference. It's given me another interest and kept me busy in a really positive way, so thank you."

If you'd like to donate to the Alana Cutland Scholarship Fund, head to justgiving.com/crowdfunding/alana-cutland

6

ANNETTE BENNY

> "Weeds are flowers too, once you get to know them."
>
> — AA MILNE

If the dictionary was to carry a picture to define the words 'positive' and 'energetic', then I am pretty sure it would be of Annette.

She lives in an idyllic spot in the middle of nowhere near Roborough in Plymouth. Home is a smallholding that was formerly a part of the larger Maristow Estate. Now, it sits, like a little island, amongst farms, grazing cows, and crops.

Having worked hard enough to retire at fifty-one, after a thirty-year career in the NHS, Annette now finds herself busier than ever, taxiing her twins around in their gap year, holding a non-executive board role, and growing her fledgling flower business.

"This wasn't how it was meant to be!" Annette jests. "I was looking forward to the girls going to university so that I'd have plenty of spare time, but I think I'll need to wait a little longer for that."

I don't like to share and burst Annette's bubble, but even when her girls have taken up whatever they intend to do after their gap years she won't have as much time as she thinks! As a mother of two daughters myself, even though they're both living in London now, I hear from them more than ever before!

"Before our call, I was taking some quiet time in the garden," Annette tells me. "I was just looking at it, thinking what I need to do, planning the tidying, getting ready for winter – just wonderful"

Like many of the people you've read about in this book, Annette wasn't ready to stop work at 51, so after six months off she found herself taking up a non-executive role with a community interest company that provides services to the NHS, something that she finds great joy in, and something that she's finding sits well beside her passion and love for flowers.

"Just before the pandemic hit, my mum and I started doing workshops at a local flower school. They were just fabulous, and we had so much fun."

"The chance came up for us both to do a professional flower-arranging course, which we jumped at. That's what we did through Covid – all online, of course, and I just loved it and became so passionate about it."

The more Annette learned about flowers and flower arranging, the more she wanted to learn more, to understand the ecology of the plants and the environmental impact caused by mass flower production. She was absolutely stunned by the information she learned, with every article throwing up something new. Annette's eyes were truly opened – and then she discovered our Cut Flower Collective group on Facebook.

"I saw the Seed to Vase course and I just thought 'oh wow, I could do this!' I knew I could grow my own."

Annette came to the course like so many others do – with no prior growing knowledge, but she did have other elements that some don't. With a veg bed prime for doubling in size and floristry skills, the piece of the puzzle that was missing was growing.

"I didn't have a clue about any of it. I knew how to create beautiful floral displays and artistic installations, but I had no clue how to start growing. I didn't know which seeds to buy, why some things work and why some don't – I was so uninformed."

Annette diligently followed the course, taking it week by week, planting, growing, and following each step. The result? A less than perfect flower patch - just how it should be!

"If I look back at the time that I was thinking about doubling the size of my vegetable patch, I remember picturing beautiful, neat beds of flowers, picture-perfect – *Instagrammable*."

"I remember being on the course and someone saying that the growing patch doesn't have to be perfect – I thought they were so wrong. But, as I stood there in late summer looking at the flower patch, I realised that I had as many nettles as I did Sunflowers and Sweet Peas, but it didn't actually matter."

"I was growing, I was producing enough flowers to create bouquets and displays, I had enough to cut for myself and enough for my mum to play with and it didn't matter how many weeds there were – nature was doing its thing and I was learning and understanding how things grow."

Growing and gardening can never be perfect. My farm never is – and that's fine. I'd rather spend time growing and making people happy with my flowers than weeding. The weeds don't hurt, and I do see them as a sign of nature doing what it should do – and we can't argue with that!

It's taken me a long time to accept that perfection is impossible, but there is always something more important to do than weeding. Even now, as I write this at the end of the year, I have a list as long as my arm of jobs to do. Flower-farming is a year-round thing, and I don't think I'll ever spend time weeding when there's so much to do!

I just do the stuff that really matters – and that's it.

"I've also learned a lot about patience," Annette says. "I've had to learn to let nature do its thing.

"Things will grow – just in their own time. Even now, in November I still have Cosmos. It's a bit battered and blown over, but there are still flowers out there."

Another thing that excites me about Annette's journey is her commitment to running a sustainable, planet-friendly business.

My dream is to see everyone with a cut flower patch, growing their own – not only would this really improve wellbeing, but it would also do the world of good for the planet.

"The more I learn, the more I can share with other people," adds Annette. "Even if it's just a small contribution, it all helps. We all need to do our bit for the planet."

Annette has started having very open conversations with clients about the ethical journey of her work and her arrangements – which is just incredible to hear.

"I set out with the idea of changing one thing to benefit the planet in every job that I did, be that using something recycled, choosing biodegradable foam, not using plastic but that's quickly turned into me being able to share with clients around five or six green benefits for each job."

"I also take the time to talk to people about their choices. When I'm asked to supply something that's out of season and must be imported, I explain the impact of their choice and very often they opt to work with seasonal, British flowers, which is just so wonderful."

Her business, Greener Gorgeous Flowers, has built up quite a following, and with a few weddings under her belt already, it would seem her community is core to everything she does.

"I set the business up quietly on Facebook and people have followed that journey. Most of my clients have come from that – there's real engagement there and I think that's so important because I don't want the flowers to just be a commodity – I want them to bring more to lives."

So, with such a strong start, where does Annette see 2022 taking her?

"I've decided that I want to focus on creating installations, which allow me to be more artistic," she tells me.

"I do some freelance work with a local florist and am part of the rota for the flowers in the local church – that's an amazing way to gain experience. I've helped her with larger-scale weddings – even one where the bride and groom took over an entire hotel! That was a real eye-opener!"

Like me, Annette has found that the physical side of flower farming is a lot more work than you'd anticipate, so she's looking forward to her husband retiring in January and joining her in the business.

I'm going to come back to a recurring theme in this chapter – and that's passion - because it really is the thread that is inter-twined in the whole of Annette's story.

"I do this because I just love tinkering with flowers," she explains to me. "I also love that beautiful flower installations bring people such joy and give them memories to treasure."

"People get a great feeling when they're around the flowers, so I want to find a way to use them to help people suffering from mental health problems; perhaps create some workshops – I'd love to see how that would work."

Combining her two passions sounds like the perfect way to explore how flowers can help with mental health and from experience, and from the other people I've spoken to for this book, I know just how growing, and 'tinkering' can benefit mental health. From ongoing anxiety to bereavement and everything in between, getting outside and digging is such a great antidote, and while it won't fix everything, it certainly helps refocus the mind – and that's wonderful.

I always tell my girls that they should do the stuff they love first – I firmly believe that if you follow your heart, you will be rewarded, and this sounds exactly like the path Annette is following, and that, well it brings me so much joy.

You can follow Annette's wonderful work at: www.facebook.com/GreenerGorgeousFlowers

7

CAROLE LAWFORD

 "Sometimes the smallest things take up the most room in your heart."

— WINNIE THE POOH

Every so often in life, something or someone comes along that completely blows you away – and for me, that person is Carole Lawford.

A former Criminal Lawyer, a medical emergency completely changed Carole's life. A diagnosis of meningitis led to a discovery of MS and the start of a whole new journey for Carole, who found herself medically retired. But still, with so much more to give, her friends and neurologist encouraged her to keep going, to start something new. So, what did Carole do? Well, this amazing woman opened her heart and set about creating an incredible community space.

Initially, the plan was to grow with a group of volunteers and build a small community focusing on flowers and vegetables, however, constraints of her allotment agreement meant that this wasn't an option…

"The council said that the allotment agreement didn't allow for more than two people to be on-site at one time, which really annoyed me – I was trying to do something good."

With a renewed determination, fuelled by her frustration, Carole took matters into her own hands, setting about creating a huge social enterprise; a place for people and community, a place for good – somewhere magical.

And so, The Hive was born.

Located in Sedgefield, The Hive is just an incredible place, but in honesty, I start the conversation with Carole with no idea of the scope and size of it. An ex-tractor and agricultural machinery showroom, the size of the place is massive. The building itself is extensive, and the garden is an incredible 600 metres square.

Inside The Hive building is a real community hub, buzzing with activity – and it's all been established by Carole, along with her amazing team of forty volunteers. And more than that – it's gone from an old, unused building to this incredible community space in just nine months. That's right – nine months – how incredible.

"Since taking the property over in January 2021, we have done so much – and I have learned an incredible amount, both in terms of growing and building a community with others."

"As a lawyer, with a lawyer's brain I'm very used to putting a task on a track and aiming for the

end, but with gardening and nature things don't happen like that – you're constantly switching tracks!"

The Hive itself is a magical place. There's a floristry workshop, a model train workshop, a community art gallery with an in-house artist, a shop, a bike exchange, and a pot sanctuary, meaning that not only is Carole doing good for the community, but it's also doing its bit for the planet.

Outside, there's more magic – and this bit excites me even more than all the things that are happening inside.

In the large garden as masses of raised beds that are used for growing flowers and veg. We'll come to the veg in a bit – this is a book about going flowers after all, so we really should start there.

"I've been cutting flowers from the cut flower patch all year – it's been wonderful," Carole continues. "We put them for sale in the shop and every day we are open, they just sell out, people adore them."

As well as public beds, tucked away past the polytunnel are Carole's own beds, which are her passion project. Having grown veg and few flowers herself in the past, she joined the Seed to Vase course in early 2021 – and, if I am frank, I am honoured that she did.

"The reward I get from growing flowers is huge," Carole said. "I have found the journey and the process so exciting, but I do still feel like I am winging it!"

"All that said, of everything I have done this year, the thing that brought me to tears with joy was seeing my incredible Café Au Lait Dahlias bloom."

"They just moved me so much, such is their beauty."

I understand this – you know, sometimes you can build huge things, but it's those amazing acts of nature, those incredible moments when Mother Earth does her thing that moves me the most. Magical doesn't even come close to describing it.

So, why does a woman as incredible as Carole sign up for a Seed to Vase course?

"For me, it gave me some structure and my own community, and I have found that so important – it was just what I needed."

"I had all these ideas flying around in my head and the course and the community, well, it gave me a tribe of people to speak to and share ideas with."

"Even on the days I was too tired to post in the groups, I was watching the community and making notes. I now have piles and piles of notebooks full of notes, all colour coordinated, which helps me to access what I need to know easily."

"The course has also helped me to understand that, instead of having one big business. I need several threads all pulling in money at the same time so that I can help it all going, supporting my volunteers, and giving the community something – it allowed me to take a strategic view of my business."

One of those threads is Carole's floristry. Her style is beautiful; whimsical, pretty, and very traditionally English, she runs classes from The Hive and, next year will take her first step into the world of weddings.

"I have had so many requests from brides who have seen my work on social media, but I have always said no – it feels like a huge responsibility, but I've agreed to take this one on, simply because I am in love with the romance of it!"

"The bride was brought up here in Sedgefield. Her wedding is here, and she wants to have flowers grown here at her wedding."

The wedding sounds like it's going to be incredible. With a marquee, it will be held in the orchard at the family farm, so there's plenty of opportunities to really display British flowers to their best.

"I have so much support around me, and I'm lucky enough that my tutor has also offered to support me when it comes to the wedding, so while I am nervous about it, I have come to realise what an honour it is to be involved."

To achieve the look and feel the bride wants to achieve, Carole will be growing flowers across three areas – but it will all be worth it as all profits will be ploughed back into the running of The Hive so that it can keep on with the good work.

"It's not only the volunteers we have a responsibility to, but we have also been feeding people and supporting by accepting donations for a charity called Feeding Families who make up Christmas hampers and distribute them as a response to the pandemic."

"We are feeding people who've lost income and family support, but we do it in such a way whereby this is a community helping each other out. It's not charity."

"This year, you might not need any help so it's good to do what you can to pay forward your good fortune, but next year you might need help, and the community is here for you – it works the other way as well. We are just about supporting each other."

The success of The Hive has already been recognised in the most magnificent way Carole could have ever wished for.

"This year – in our first year – we were nominated for an **RHS** *In Your Neighbourhood* Award. We didn't have massive expectations, after all, we are still very much 'under development', and we aimed at achieving a Level 1 award."

"We felt that was the most we could hope for – and we were excited for that – being given a Level 1 award meant that we'd have somewhere to aim next year, but somehow we managed to achieve the highest level – a Level 5, with an outstanding recommendation also. I was blown away."

In fact, it turns out the **RHS** were blown away as well, having never had a first-time entry achieve such a high level.

"One of the judges came to me and told me that they had to check the rule book because we scored so highly, and they weren't sure if we could have the award!"

"I am so proud of us achieving that award – but more than that, I am so proud of all of the volunteers who rallied around and made everything look beautiful for the judges. I am so proud of all their hard work and so incredibly proud of what The Hive gives to our community."

"We were all so overwhelmed. When I reflect and I think about the friends we have all made, the difference we've made – to the lives of others and our own, I am blown away."

See – I told you she was incredible – and just wait until you hear the plans for 2022.

First up is the installation of a kitchen which will allow people to come along, pick fresh veg, prepare it and the turn it into a nutritious meal. Then, once the enterprise has been given the official nod, the Hive will open ten more beds in the outdoor space.

These beds will specifically be reserved for people living with Alzheimer's and Dementia, providing a space for them to grow, achieve and get outside in a safe, supportive atmosphere. Just amazing!

"I just want to reach as many people as we can," Carole finishes.

Carole's story is beyond inspiring, to have been through what she has and to decide to open her heart and use it for good to help others is just the most wonderful act of selflessness I have ever seen.

Although she would no doubt credit it to her friends and team, I think someone needs to nominate this woman for an MBE – like her flowers, she really is the best of British.

8

DEBORAH O'CONNOR

 "If the string breaks, then we try another piece of string."

— OWL

Based in Bishopstone, near Aylesbury, Deborah O'Connor is a florist-turned-grower who was already growing many of her own blooms before starting the Seed to Vase course. However, even with her prior knowledge, Deborah has learned an incredible amount through the tutorials and talks, and it's changed her whole outlook on floristry and the flower industry.

Since being made redundant from Marks and Spencer at the age of 28, Deborah has followed the well-trodden path of a high street florist, achieving her qualifications, opening two London-based shops, before reluctantly closing them and downsizing to more rural Buckinghamshire. She now runs her business from her workshop – the converted garage at her house that overlooks her garden where she grows as many flowers as she can.

She signed up to the Seed to Vase course not knowing quite what to expect – with such a long-established career in floristry and already growing her own, Deborah herself will be the first to share how much she's learned.

"I grew all the seeds that came to me as part of the course – in fact, I still have flowers coming up now in November – which is marvellous. I have also had my eyes opened to trying to be more environmentally friendly."

Moving towards a more planet-friendly way of producing bouquets and displays is something I feel that the flower industry is behind on. For example, let's look at the oasis that florists use. You can now buy a partially biodegradable oasis, but it's still not good enough – and eco-friendly alternatives to oasis and cellophane are often cost-prohibitive to smaller florists.

"My husband thinks I am mad because I keep signing up to courses like this, having also recently done a marketing course, but I think it's very important to learn new things every day and I just want to keep my brain ticking over!"

"I have been arranging flowers for over 30 years and over that time I've always done it in the way I've been taught City and Guilds, adding in my own individual style - but this course has made me see things with new eyes, I'm not afraid to do things a little differently now and to step away from being quite so struc-tured, introducing a more free-flowing natural style"

Now, with a greenhouse installed, Deborah is ready to go for 2022, intending to use as many of her own-grown flowers as much as possible.

"I am committed to making sure that I can make growing British seasonal flowers work for the business," she tells me. "I want to use more British Flowers in my arrangements, and I want to lower my carbon footprint as much as I can."

As I have shared with you in my introduction, many of the flowers we see in supermarkets, florists and garage forecourts are flown to the United Kingdom across many thousands of miles from far-flung destinations such as Africa and Columbia. Even during the year of the pandemic, Columbia exported a massive 660 million stems, with Kenya supplying one-third of all roses sold in the EU.[1]

Every 12,000 rose stems grown in Kenya incur a carbon footprint of 2,200kg CO_2[2] - multiply that by the eight million stems that made their way to the UK for Valentine's Day in 2017[3], and you can see the problem.

"I want to cut down purchasing from international suppliers as much as I can," Deborah tells me when we get onto talking about climate change. "I can't keep buying from them - I feel guilty when I hear people saying the things they're doing for the planet, and I want to do more - I am just not there yet, but I am trying."

"So, my plan for next year is to grow more seasonal British flowers, cut my carbon footprint and save myself a bit of money too!"

The last two years have brought Deborah the respite to get to know her garden better. Furloughed from her other part-time job during the lockdown, she found peace in her outdoor space, just like so many of us have done.

"I have discovered that I am happiest when I am working in the garden. This last year has been such a great year - it's been so nice to potter around – the lockdown allowed me to do more of the things I love doing – and I loved that!'

'It's changed my life – even my husband says I am more relaxed and overall, I just feel more content in myself. It's a wonderful feeling."

Deborah's de-stressing in the garden completely chimes with me. If I am feeling overwhelmed or stressed, I just step outside and plant some seeds – it's such a fabulous way to de-stress and unwind.

"I just want to grow flowers now," she adds. "You know, I believe that you have to do what feels right because you're only here for a short time – and that's the motto I intend to live my life by."

I get that too!

The key to being a successful flower farmer is all in the planning, something the Seed to Vase programme helps would-be growers with – it's even helpful for those who already have a rough idea of what they're doing, like Deborah.

"The course has taught me so much and being a part of the Facebook page community is just wonderful - everyone is so lovely and helpful," she continued.

"I want to use more of the flowers I grow in 2022, without question. I did want to use more in 2021, but I just didn't quite get the timings right – next year will be different."

"I only have a small cottage front garden, which is where I do all of my growing, but I intend to take full advantage of every inch of the space."

So, what else is on the agenda for Deborah in 2022?

"More floristry, more teaching, and more sharing the joys of British flowers."

"I already run wreath-making classes, but I am working on a more structured timetable so that I can run classes right throughout the year. I'd also love to teach people how to grow their own stems and learn how to arrange them too."

With such a long-established career in floristry, Deborah has a chance here to help push real change through in the flower world, to influence how things move into the future – and that makes me so happy!

---

1. *Source: ideasted.com
2. Source: Cranfield University
3. Source: cityam.com

9

DIANE & ROGER DANGELL

> "So wherever I am, there's always Pooh,
>
> There's always Pooh and Me.
>
> "What would I do?" I said to Pooh,
>
> "If it wasn't for you," and Pooh said to me: "True,
>
> It isn't much fun for One, but Two
>
> Can stick together," says Pooh, says he.
>
> "That's how it is," says Pooh."
>
> — A.A. MILNE, NOW WE ARE SIX

Throughout this book there are lots of stories about how people joined the Seed to Vase course for all sorts of reasons; to help with mental health, to start a business, to relieve stress - and while everyone that has grown with us has found joy, there aren't very many people who sign up 'just because' – but, Diane and Roger Dangell are an exception to that rule.

The story of this couple from Hertfordshire is just adorable. They're true soul mates. Having met through work, with Roger in a career as a Consultant Engineer and Diane an Accountant, they've been together ever since!

Having taken early retirement from their busy professional lives in 2019, once their boys had finished University, Roger and Diane found themselves with plenty of time on their hands – and even more when the pandemic hit.

"Before we retired, we had worked together for twelve years," Diane laughed as she continued. "Thanks to white wine, we'd adapted quite nicely to being together twenty-four/seven, so retirement came easily to us."

Since moving into their house twenty-seven years ago, the pair have been non-stop. After an epic 18-year restoration project, they were able to turn their attention to the wonderfully large garden that came with the house

"Over the years we developed an interest in gardening - we have gradually transformed the garden from a football pitch for the boys, and have added beds and even a swimming pool, which is wonderful," Diane continued.

"In the early days, we used to buy plants from the Gardening Club stall at the village fete because they were cheaper than the garden centres. Over time, we gained a reputation with the Gardening Club members for committing plant genocide!"

"You could almost hear the plants screaming as we took them home! Slowly we learned that plants and shrubs needed to be nurtured in time with the seasons and had needs, like water and sunlight, and that they don't always adjust to where you put them."

I love this story because I know where their journey has taken them – but more of that to come!

As well as being novice gardeners, Diane and Roger are also keen travellers, but as everyone knows, the global pandemic put paid to all of that.

"With Covid came the cancellation of our early retirement long haul travel plans, which was a shame. Our boys were off making their own lives - one in Canada and one in London - so we were really at a loose end, which was very strange."

"Instead of our long-planned long-haul trip, we spent three weeks travelling around Somerset, Devon, and Cornwall in September 2020, visiting gardens, tea shops, and nice restaurants – it was glorious – and it was at this point we decided to expand our beds and create a cut flower patch."

And so, after years of misplaced planting and committing "plant genocide", Diane and Roger's cut flower journey was born.

"I love having flowers in the house," Diane continued. "So, it seemed sensible to have a bash at growing our own – and it gave us a new project to focus on."

Diane and Roger followed the course to the tee – and took it to the next level. Now, with a 50m bed at the bottom of their garden, the most high-tech irrigation system I've seen in a long while, and a long-forgotten reputation as plant-killers, the cut flower course has been an absolute revelation to the couple – bringing them immense joy.

Of course, the journey wasn't easy for them – there were plenty of mistakes on the way, after all - a reputation as a plant killer takes some time to repair! I followed their journey keenly through the eight months of the course through the gardener's diary everyone completed and saw them go through highs and lows. I enjoyed their stories of nursing back seedlings in their own 'intensive care unit' (aka their home gym), by propping them up with cocktail sticks – so resourceful, and they were just dedicated to becoming good plant parents.

· · ·

"Looking after seedlings proved to be quite problematic - mainly due to a lack of experience and some silly mistakes. We also suffered some confidence issues when the potting on went wrong but after a couple of days of nursing most recovered."

"That said, we have learned so much – and can't wait to expand what we are doing next year."

To say Diane and Roger learned a lot would be an understatement. They now spend hours in the garden planting, relaxing, and enjoying retirement. They've had lots of success with their flowers, despite their confidence knocks and Roger has become the King of Irrigation, having installed a complex system that he can control at the touch of his smartphone from wherever he is in the world. Entirely intuitive to the weather and humidity, it really is a thing of beauty, and the most incredible system I've heard of in the garden of an amateur grower.

Roger's engineering skills, along with patience and the fact that they threw themselves fully into the course means that the couple are ready to take their cut flower patch to the next level in 2022.

Their newly built 50 metre bed is set to be expanded – 50 metres is huge already, so I can't wait to see how far they go!

Fitter, happy and healthy, for this wonderful couple the joy of gardening comes from sharing their flowers with friends and family. Roger's sister received the most beautiful bouquet of Dahlias, and visitors to the house very rarely leave without a bunch of beautiful British fresh-cut flowers.

This joy is something I feel every time a bride walks into the decorated venue for her wedding, or I see the results of a group member's growth. Flowers bring so much joy – which is just another reason I want everyone in the UK to grow their own cut flower patch and, as Diane and Roger have shown, doing it for absolute and pure joy is something wonderful. Bringing pleasure to them and their friends and family is the greatest gift, it really is! That and relieving them of their plant killer reputation, of course!

10

DONNA SELLICK

"Doing nothing often leads to the very best of something"

— A.A. Milne, Winnie The Pooh

Having had a career in hospitality for all her adult life (and some of her younger years), it was the passing of her father from Covid-19 in 2020 that spurred Donna Sellick on to make a complete life change.

Having promised her father that she would use any inheritance to work less and live more, she decided to ditch the 14-hour days, and instead follow a different path – *to stop and smell the roses*.

Now, with her fledgling business Busy B Blooms beginning to take flight, Donna describes herself as "trying to be a flower person", which, honestly, is an entirely modest way, to sum up, her journey so far.

"When my Dad died in 2020, he left some money and I promised him that I would use it in order to work less," Kent-based Donna told me.

"At around the same time, my husband became poorly and required kidney dialysis. As my job took me in and out of schools, I was incredibly worried about bringing Covid home to him, so I decided to jump off the wagon."

"Swapping one devil for another" is how Donna describes her leap from her role as a professional caterer into the world of flower farming – and, yes, I can understand that.

"I was on the road a lot in my old job. I'd leave the house at 5.30 am and get back at 7 pm, and it was a tough gig. It was a great gig, but the time came to jump out, so I did."

"That said, I knew that even though I had stopped working in my lifelong career, I had more in me - I knew that I could do another job, that I could create something else – I wasn't ready to completely stop!"

Donna found her way to my course in the same way as so many others have; she "fell down the rabbit hole of Instagram", and before she knew it, she was signed up to the Seed to Vase course and a whole host of others, attending weekly talks and sessions and learning the ways of farming British blooms. The rest, as they say, is a fabulous story in the making.

"Once I got the bug, I set my intention that I was going to grow some flowers and, if I managed to arrange them and sell some on the way, brilliant – it would help fund my flower addiction!"

The last two years have been an emotional rollercoaster of epic proportions for Donna, but thankfully she's had yoga and her garden to keep her sane – but, once she'd stopped working it didn't take long for her to get itchy feet.

"Unfortunately, after so many years leading a professional life, you're wired to do everything to the best of your ability – it's difficult to just play at something."

And so began the seeds of Donna's business began to germinate.

"I didn't set out with this in mind, but in the blink of an eye, I was building a brand, having a logo designed, setting up an Instagram page, and now, I am on this journey, and I am learning something new every day."

One of the biggest shifts for Donna has been getting used to the world of social media and harnessing the benefits it has for her business.

"Instagram is a full-time job in itself, isn't it?" Something I completely agree with, as I spend around 20 hours a week creating and sharing content. "I went from never posting anything to my old boss telling me that she thought I was the queen of Instagram."

"Perhaps a princess in training, but no, not a queen!"

Of course, moving from the corporate hospitality world and into the unreliable world of flower farming with all its uncontrollables is a massive step. You never really know what weather you're waking up to, or whether all those dahlia tubers you've lovingly planted and cared for will turn into beautiful, saleable stems -something that Donna has really had to wrap her head around, while still retaining the life balance she has sought for so long.

"It goes without saying, but the work is a lot more than I am used to physically – and the uncontrollables are different. If it's not snails nibbling at things, it's something else. But I still love it!"

"Also, trying to keep everything growing in an eco-friendly way is a lot of work, it's the right thing to do, but it's a lot more work than you'd anticipate."

Right now, Donna's business is still very much in its infancy. Undoubtedly, she has been nibbled herself by the flower farming snail and admits to, "buying a stupid number of dahlias and planting lots of tulips and planning what to grow for the future" but she still doesn't know which direction this will take her.

With an allotment plot prepped for spring and borders in her garden, Donna is already shaping the future of her business, however, that looks. With Pinterest boards and ideas already in formation for her own 'whimsical' collection of bouquets and floral displays and the vast knowledge provided by the Seed to Vase course, she has everything she needs.

"My style isn't structured. I like to make my bouquets and displays look and feel whimsical, with that country feel, showing off those British flowers at their best."

Confidence plays a big part in setting up any new business, and I work to make sure the Seed to Vase course gives people the self-belief and knowledge to grow it.

I firmly believe that this is the right time for Donna – and so many others like her – to take this step into making flower farming their business, their career. There are so many factors in play right now that make this the right time to get growing.

Putting aside how romantic and delightful a bouquet of British seasonal flowers looks, there are just so many different elements that are making UK flowers more appealing than ever to florists.

When I first started flower farming at Field Gate Flowers, high street and local florists simply weren't interested in buying buckets of flowers from me regularly. They were enjoying low-cost imported flowers, grown thousands of miles away, blissfully unaware of the environmental impact their blooms were causing.

Now, post-Brexit and in the wake of COP26, I am finding that florists are more open-minded to working with seasonal British flowers. Of course, this is probably largely down to the fact that at the time of writing imported flowers have increased by around forty percent in the last twelve months – a huge cost for any business to bear.

Perhaps one way forward for Donna, which would allow her to retain some work-life balance while developing the business and fulfilling her flower addiction would be to sell directly to florists – especially as we all become more conscious about how we shop and the journey of what we buy.

"I am all set for 2022 – by that I mean I've got everything planned to grow and have a way forward," she continued. "I am going to see how the year goes and go from there."

Of course, you can't put a price on the love and support of family and friends too – especially when it comes to sharing the good word about your business and the virtues of buying locally grown seasonal, cut-to-order flowers.

"You know, I am really lucky that I am already receiving orders," Donna continued. "My friends and family have been wonderful – and everyone just adores how gorgeous the flowers are."

Moving into a new career in middle age is, without doubt, a daunting notion, but I am wholly confident that Donna has many of the skills and attributes she needs already to make it work. Most importantly, she really isn't afraid of hard work – and that is something that's inherent – that can't be taught through an online course.

I'll be keeping an eye on Busybblooms over the next year or so to see where it takes Donna – I'm sure wherever it takes her, she will do a fabulous job and do the flowers she grows justice.

11

FIONA BODDY

 "I always get to where I'm going by walking away from where I have been."

— WINNIE THE POOH

Sometimes in life, you just need to close your eyes and take a leap of faith. Sometimes, you need to just dive in, go with your gut, believe in yourself, and jump – which is exactly what Fiona Boddy has done over the last year.

Since moving back from New Zealand, Fiona and her husband, Hugh, who live between Harrogate and York, have owned land. They've often wondered how to make it profitable, so, with a penchant for beautiful flowers and masses of encouragement from Hugh, Fiona went for it.

"I just felt so isolated in lockdown," Fiona tells me as we chat from our respective sofas. "My brain was numb, and I was desperate for some stimulation."

"I needed something to get my teeth into, something to throw my heart into."

"I've always loved flower arranging – I'm not an expert, but I have always had a real interest and Hugh has always thought I could make a career of it, so with his push I just went for it!"

So, with her land ready to go, Fiona set about building her business. Intending to start off with one bed, Fiona's leap of faith went into hyper-drive.

"The timing was right and things all just started to connect up."

"When we were putting in the first bed, I realised that it would probably be not too much more work to put ten beds in, so I went for it."

"Wow! Just wow! This is brilliant! In my first year, I worked with three beds, and I found that quite enough."

"Yes, I did find the growing quite overwhelming – and for me, that was the biggest challenge for the first few months."

"I knew nothing about growing and here I was, having never grown anything more than a few lettuces from a packet trying to grow lots of different types of flowers – and not only growing but trying to grow to establish a business!"

"It was hard, but the biggest frustration for me was that I felt that I was constantly working into a vacuum, not knowing if what I was doing was the right thing. We'd put some solid investment into the business – the beds, the compost, the irrigation – we really committed."

"It was very stressful."

"And then I connected with the course and the community – it was the missing piece, and it gave me the confidence to step into the flower journey fully."

Flowers and gardening are meant to be good for mental health – they're not meant to cause stress, but I get how Fiona felt. In the beginning, when there's nothing there but a bed of mud and manure and you just have seeds in the ground you don't know what's going to happen – you just have to hope it works – and that can be scary!

I am glad that the Seed to Vase course gave Fiona the all-important final piece of the puzzle; confidence – that was always my hope for everyone who signed up, but never did I dream that there would be someone who could establish themselves in the industry so well within just seven months. At that speed, it's no wonder it was so stressful!

"Even in the first few months of going, I had no real idea about what I was working towards. I didn't know how many flowers I would grow, how I was going to sell them, and how it was going to go."

"One night, I woke up in a cold sweat worrying that my Amaranthus hadn't taken, so I ordered about thirty plugs. It turns out that my Amaranthus was just slow – once they started, and the plugs took I ended up with acres of the things!"

One of the things that many people who join the cut flower course share with me is how wonderfully supportive they find the community we've managed to build – and Fiona attributes this to getting her through those first weeks and months.

"Everyone on the course is just so, so supportive," she continued. "I could ask any question and within minutes I had a response and an answer – the Cut Flower Collective community was such a lifesaver."

From bare paddocks in spring to launching in August, Fiona has had a phenomenal first season and I can express just how proud I am of her. Now, well-established in her locale, I am so excited to see what happens next.

"After the beds went down in May, we started planning for the launch. I managed to get a website built, my Instagram page up and running, flyers produced and get it out there."

"We ended up with around 80 people popping along, which was lovely. It was such a fab day. Some people stayed and chatted for hours, some bought bouquets, and everyone wanted to know more about the flowers and the principles behind why growing and cutting British blooms are best for the planet."

"We have had such a successful season," Fiona continues. "Ouseburn Meadows Flower Farm is now firmly on the map, and we have a good little income."

"But I know that next year will be so much easier – I know have knowledge that I didn't have last year, and we now have the infrastructure for growing established."

With customers already buying from Fiona, the next year does indeed look exciting, with plans for workshops, providing sustainable floral solutions for funerals and even more growing, but it's not just about the commercial side of things. As well as beautiful, sustainable flowers, her journey has grown something far, far more important.

"When I started on this journey, I wanted to find a way to build a community around the flowers."

"When we first started selling, I noticed that the people coming to buy bouquets and bunches were newly widowed or new to the village; people looking for a community. People were coming out of lockdown and wanted to reconnect again, and I found that, quite organically, we were starting to build a community."

"I am now joined regularly by a small bunch of volunteers who come along and help me. I have some who help with the dead-heading, some come and make the teas and coffees at events. There's always lots of chatter and support for each other."

"It's such a hearty community – everyone supports and helps each other – it's just so wonderful to see and to be a part of."

Goodness! Fiona's story is just breath-taking. How she has created a business from a standing start in far less than a year is just amazing, and I am so proud to know that the Seed to Vase course has played a part in her journey.

I often tell fledgling flower farmers that it will take time to make money and that the first three years are hard – but Fiona is clearly the exception to the rule, and I just cannot wait to see what happens next! I just hope that I can keep up.

www.ouseburnmeadows.co.uk

https://www.facebook.com/profile.php?id=100063457537643

@ouseburnmeadows

12

HEATHER HARRIS

 "How lucky am I to have something that makes saying goodbye so hard."

— WINNIE THE POOH

With life expectancy higher than ever before it is no surprise that, for so many people, once retirement hits, they feel that they still have plenty left to give. For some, this might mean taking on childcare duties for their grandchildren, others might volunteer or work part-time – but for some, it can give them the chance to fulfil an un-explored ambition.

Meet Heather. Paediatric nurse, one of the UK's incredible army of vaccinators, and the wife of a farmer, who lives in glorious Dartmouth with her husband, son, and her amazing 97-year-old father who lives down the road from her.

Living on a working farm is a lifestyle that takes some work – especially one as productive at Glebe farm, which produces beef, pork,chicken, and lamb. But in amongst all the work and farming, Heather has managed to find herself a little patch to call her own.

Tucked away in the farm's orchard, during 2020 the land Heather has seconded was used to produce veg, but in 2021 it was turned over to flowers, starting Heather on her cut-flower journey.

"I lost my mother to Dementia a few years ago and she was a wonderful gardener -she had the most gorgeous cottage garden full of peonies and roses," she tells me. "I've always worked as a nurse for the NHS so mum used to do my garden for me, but since I stopped working, I decided I wanted to give growing my own cut flowers a go."

With time on her hands, Heather immersed herself in her new hobby, taking a cut flower course and a floristry course at Dartington Hall, which was complemented by following the Grow Girls Podcast, a subscrip-tion to the Floral Project, and then a sign up to our cut flower course and the Growth for Business course. What a journey!

So, converting a veg patch into a cut flower patch is quite some work – but, thankfully, Heather discovered the Charles Dowding no-dig method, which I just love.

For the uninitiated, let me tell you a bit about the no-dig method. Developed by Charles in his Somerset garden since the 1980s, it involves, as you'd imagine – no digging. Instead, beds are created using cardboard, compost, and manure. The hope is that the beds remain weed-free, making them perfect for growing flowers, fruit, or veg. It is a marvellous technique –

but it can be expensive if you don't have access to plenty of manure and if you're doing it over a large space.

"My neighbours all thought I was mad!" Heather laughs. "I was constantly asking for cardboard, using manure we have here, asking for any wood chip – but it did the trick!"

Part of the cut flower course we run recommends that participants take a photo diary of their journey. Not only does this help them to see their progress, but the diary also lets them see what went wrong, what went well, and what the following year needs to make it better than the last.

"The biggest disaster for me has to be the huge number of slugs and snails I get- there are just so many! Oh – and my cats. I have four and they've been particularly unhelpful – unlike the diary – that's been incredibly constructive."

This year has been a little bumpy and busy for Heather to say the least. Between supporting her elderly father, setting up a glamping site on the farm and a car accident that left her with whiplash it's a wonder she's managed to find the time and energy to turn flower farming into a small business already - but she has.

"My wonderful son built me a cupboard at the farm gate. I used that to sell tin can arrangements and bunches of sweet peas. That went well, but there are reflections I can take forward to improve things next year."

"From there, I moved on to other regular little jobs. I created a weekly flower display for the local bistro, made arrangements for Dartmouth tearooms, and I even did some adorable little pumpkin flower displays for the quiz night of the Dartmouth food festival – they were popular."

"I've also done the flowers for a sixtieth birthday party in a marquee and have had some inquiries about weddings next year – I'm not making tonnes of money, but I am making enough to buy more seeds and more bulbs, which is just great."

"That said, I do think that maybe I missed a trick this year."

"I took tentative steps – I didn't know how many flowers I would have so I didn't print business cards. Looking back now, I do wish that I had, because the bistro and the food festival received lots of inquiries about where their displays had come from."

I suppose the next step for Heather is to decide where she wants this journey to take her. How much does she want to do? Where does she want to head? Who is she aiming her produce at? The real joy with flower farming is that you can scale it to whatever works for you. Go big or stay small – it doesn't matter - it's all about the pleasure you get from it.

"I'm not going for big business," Heather added. "I'll stick to being a hobbyist floral arranger, I think – but we will see!"

Having been a professional person her whole life, Heather has no desire to settle down into being a farmer's wife any time soon and, if I am completely honest, I can't imagine her sticking to being a hobbyist flower farmer either.

"I was driving from a friend's house in the summer, and I saw this beautiful strip of sunflowers. They looked incredible, and I know I could do the same. Sunflowers are so popular around here and they're so easy to grow, so I am probably going to give those a go for 2022."

See what I mean? I don't think flowers will be just a hobby for long!

Heather is so enterprising – she's completely inspirational. To achieve what she has this year in the face of everything else she has going on is no mean feat – what a woman. I can't help but wonder what's next.

13

ISOBEL HOLLOWAY

 "Sometimes, the smallest things take up the most room in your heart"

— WINNIE THE POOH

I caught up with Isobel on a dark November evening after she'd spent the day in the garden planting a massive 120 tulip bulbs. Coincidentally, on the day we spoke, I'd also spent the day doing the same – the gardener's diary, eh?

I first met Isobel when she joined the Seed to Vase course. With a huge garden, she persuaded her husband to dig a number of beds for her on their front lawn, creating three small circular beds and a larger one - big enough to house the 120 tulips, planted in a starburst formation ready to bloom in incredible fashion next spring.

A city girl born and bred just a mile away from Coronation Street gardening and growing aren't things that Isobel had been brought up with – however when she went to university that changed. Finding herself in a more rural location, she got into gardening, growing perennials, and her own vegetables.

When she joined the Seed to Vase course, Isobel was no stranger to the world of horticulture. She currently works at Wakehurst – an incredible botanical garden in Sussex that is part of the Kew Gardens collection. With more than 500 acres of plants, trees and wildlife and the national Millennium Seed Bank housed there, Isobel is a member of the Kew teaching programme, spending her days enthusing primary school children about plants and the natural world around them.

"It's just the most magical place," Isobel told me. "When I am there early in the morning and we head out to gather petals and pond dip ahead of the young visitors arriving, it's wonderful. Hearing the birds, listening to the rustling – there's nothing like it!"

"It brings me such peace."

The benefits of gardening when it comes to coping with stress and mental health issues cannot be overstated. I find immense peace when I am in the garden or walking the dog – there's nowhere else I would find that same level of tranquillity – it's something so wonderful.

"I did some gardening when the children were younger and at school," Isobel adds. "I can honestly say it's the only time I could have forgotten to pick them up from school, so yes – I agree – gardening does help you completely switch off!"

Isobel's motivation to step into the world of growing flowers to cut is very different from most of the other people I've spoken to curate the chapters in this book. She's on this journey purely for pleasure, which is just perfect – but there's also a little more to it.

"My daughter will be getting married in early 2022," she tells me. "She requested natural confetti for her day, so I started researching how I could grow the flowers to do that and that's how I found the Seed to Vase course."

Already, Isobel has learned enough to be able to help with creating some of the displays and flower adornments for her daughter's wedding – but that's come with its own challenges.

"You need a lot of flowers for natural confetti," Isobel laughs. "And I have also discovered that pink petals turn yellow!"

"Our garden is also on a slope, so growing straight stems has been somewhat of a challenge – and, living in Sussex, we've really had to prime the beds for growing, mixing fine compost in with the clay soil by hand to create optimum growing conditions for everything."

"And the slugs, the slugs are a nightmare!"

"The only way we can deal with the slugs is manually! Every night my husband is out there with a headtorch, moving them on, making sure they don't attack our flowers. Some nights we have had as many as one hundred and twenty to deal with!"

Ahead of the wedding, Isobel's house has turned into a makeshift nursery, with *seedlings everywhere – it's like March!*

She has managed to salvage and dry some homegrown lavender, which has retained its beautiful true-blue hue, and is expecting lots of Snow Drops and White Muscari but preparing for a late winter wedding is undoubtedly going to be tricky.

"I really don't want to have to buy flowers, so we're really thinking about how we can work with the green and white theme of the wedding's floral, and foliage displays."

Bringing your flowers and displays to a wedding as part of the day is a very special honour. Whether you're doing it as a paid commission or adding something magical to a family wedding, it's a wonderful thing to do, but also a lot of pressure.

Every year my team and I deal with both small and large-scale weddings, and while these are some of the most gorgeous events to create for, each booking has high expectations – especially, when like me, you want to create as near to perfection as possible.

Recently we did the flowers and foliage for a wedding for a bride who was celebrating on her parent's land. The marquee was beautiful (I love marquee weddings as they allow us the be really creative). The service was in a local church, the church where the bride went when she was little, so it really meant something to her. It took a team of six of us four days to create all the floral decorations. There was a flower arch at the reception along with beautiful foliage hoops, and we also decorated the whole church. It was great fun.

But a wedding is about so much more than the flowers and foliage - we have ironed tablecloths at venues, we've helped the bride sort her dress out and made dashes for forgotten bouquets- we will do whatever it takes to make the wedding perfect – and while those expectations aren't a part of the contract, they are the things I need to add to do justice to the beautiful flowers we grow.

"I did offer to do most of the flowers for the wedding," Isobel tells me. "But my daughter and I chatted, deciding that we would rather that I played my part in the day instead of worrying, so I will be providing lots of the additional flowers instead.

"You wouldn't believe the number of jam jars I have in the house ready for the wedding! I've also grown lots of Ivies and have bought a Weeping Willow, which hopefully will yield some beautiful silver catkins for me to use."

So, what's next for Isobel? Well, after growing everything that came as part of the Seed to Vase course with some success, she's raring to go for next year.

"I will not be giving up! I've already bought my seeds for next year and I fully intend to keep growing – but I will be planting more annuals."

"But I won't be planting tulips next year!"

I suspect that when Isobel sees the results of her hard day's planting, she will change her mind on that last one. For me, the first tulips that bloom each year are a sign of something beautiful coming. They bring such joy and such optimism – I am sure Isobel will enjoy the benefits of her day's planting far longer than that it takes her to recover from it!

"One thing that has been wonderful for me is the fact that my girls are also starting to come around to getting out in the garden – that brings me such joy."

This is something that brings me huge pleasure also. Seeing young people start to engage in what has traditionally been the preserve of the retired is just fabulous. As I mentioned earlier in this chapter, the benefits to mental health and general wellbeing that gardening and being in nature can bring are not to be underestimated – and certainly should be capitalised on by younger people in their busy, screen-led lives.

I am so looking forward to seeing the results of Isobel's growing efforts when the photographs of her daughter's wedding wing their way over to me. For me, the Seed to Vase course is about so much; it's not just about opening up a business opportunity for those looking for a new way of life, it's about being able to create special moments and bringing joy to others – and that's just so special.

14

JENNIE PEACHEY

" "Don't underestimate the value of Doing Nothing, of just going along, listening to all the things you can't hear, and not bothering."

— WINNIE THE POOH

One of my favourite books that I've read in recent times is a book called 'Rushing Woman's Syndrome'. In it, the writer, Dr Libby Weaver, talks about the impact of the never-ending to-do list and how to stay healthy amongst it all.

I have rushing woman's syndrome – and I see it also in the lovely Jennie, who joined the cut flower course in spring 2021.

A busy, busy working mother, with a son in the middle of his GCSEs, she is constantly on the go. If she's not at work, she's running, cycling, walking the dog, or doing something else.

"I'm not very good at slowing down," she tells me as we chat. "We fill our lives to the max!"

Tell me about it!

Jennie, her husband Ed and her son Thomas moved to Berkhamsted ten years ago having spent many years travelling the world, living in Istanbul, Dublin, and Shanghai. Once their house, a glorious restoration project took shape, ten years ago, Jennie and her husband had their garden landscaped and had three raised beds installed. The beds were intended to play host to veg and cut flowers – the veg came to fruition, but the cut flowers – well, they've taken a while longer.

"I've always tinkered with flowers in the garden, changing up my tubs and pots, but I'd never really look anything up or take it any further."

Jennie finally took the plunge and started a cut flower course back in September 2020, which inspired her to learn more about growing and cutting flowers. Then I appeared in her Facebook feed!

"I have a wonderful friend, Julie, who has extensive knowledge of flowers. She could name any flower -but I had no idea what they were, and I wanted to know more!"

"When I signed up to the course, I knew nothing," Jennie tells me. "And, if I am honest, I was a little hesitant at signing up - we've all had so much screen time over the last couple of years - I wasn't sure if I wanted to commit myself to more, but the great thing about the course is that you don't have to commit to a certain time or place - everything is there forever to pick up and use whenever you need it, and that's been brilliant."

So, starting in the same way as I did, with three raised beds in her garden, Jennie set about growing her own cut flowers – five years after the beds were installed.

As we spoke, I got the impression that Jennie was somewhat of a perfectionist, making her flower-growing journey a little more difficult than others found it.

"Yes, I am quite competitive," she admits. "I'd get a little frustrated when I saw the progression of others in the group. I had all these seeds planted and they weren't germinating – or so I thought. In fact, they were just slow to germinate."

If I had a Dahlia tuber for every time I've told someone that gardening has no rhyme or reason and that there's very little that is predictable when it comes to flower farming, I'd have enough Dahlias to fill every vase in the UK - but it's true. The weather, the climate, unpredictable cold snaps, warm spells - it doesn't take much to throw things out of kilter, and that's probably the hardest part of all of this, accepting failure and learning that it's ok.

You also need to be selective in terms of what you want to learn and know. You don't have to know everything about growing flowers to grow enough to create bouquets for all your friends and family – I certainly don't know everything about every flower, insect, and weed, but I know enough, and that's all anyone needs to know! It also needs to be fun, that's the most important bit - life's too short to do anything that you don't find fun!

But, regardless of slow germinating seeds, Jennie ended up with a beautiful bed of 'random blooms' ("random suits me", she throws in), and her garden has become somewhat of a sanctuary, giving her time and space to slow down – a blessing during late summer.

"My mum was always brilliant in the garden – it was absolutely her happy place," she continues. "She seemed to know exactly what to do and when, but I didn't take anything in, and that's something I regret now – I wish I could just pick up the phone and ask her questions."

In September, Jennie's mum passed away with cancer. She'd spent her last months in a care home which, as Jennie told me, was surrounded by the most beautiful gardens and woodland area – it's a very special place for the patients who all suffer from neurological problems. Since then, she has realised how much peace and tranquillity that gardening can bring, and how wonderful the slowing down and the quiet can be.

When I am in the greenhouse or sowing in one of the beds, I find it gives me the space to stop, think and take a step back, because there's nothing else to do. When I'm up to my elbows in soil I need to focus and take my time – and that is a real blessing – in fact, I get annoyed when someone disturbs me! I like the solitary time – and that's been quite the lesson to learn for me!

So, how do the next twelve months look for Jennie?

"I need to stop and make a plan," she tells me. Of course! This is Jennie after all!

"My wonderful friend Julie has been planting her Dahlia tubers and planning what she's growing next year, but I'm not quite at that stage – but I'll get there."

Having taken half an allotment patch next to her friend, I think Jennie might have finally found that time to slow down and stop rushing – but I'm keen to find out whether this is going to become more than just a hobby.

"When I first started growing, I intended to take bouquets into the care home where Mum lived and to give them out to other patients and the staff as a thank you. Unfortunately, Covid put paid to that, but I am going to do something with the flowers to raise money for the centre, because everyone there is just incredible, and I need to give back to them for everything they did for Mum."

How gorgeous! What better way to give back than by spreading joy with stunning British flowers? I am sure that beautiful bouquets sold for charity will be very popular – even I'd buy one!

"I feel very ready to get planning for next year," Jennie continues. "I have my little plot at the allotment, and I feel like I have learned so much from the course."

"When I started, I knew nothing at all - I was a total beginner, but now I know so much more – and the things I don't know, well, I am happy to look them up and I'm more inclined to learn, the course has given me the confidence to know that I can do this."

And what of the original three beds?

"We missed our fresh salad and veg this year," she tells me. "So, they'll be used for growing vegetables this year and my annuals will live at the allotment – although, our garden is quite spacious, so there is plenty of room for me to grow my perennials, shrubs, roses, and peonies"

15

JULIE SMITH

 "A day without a friend is like a pot without a single drop of honey left inside"

— WINNIE THE POOH

You know, I quite enjoy a good Zoom chat. For me, over the last 18 months, I have come to realise that you can get to know someone just as well virtually as you can by meeting them in real life. Since the lifting of restrictions, there are many people I've met in real life who I've only met virtually previously, and it doesn't feel like a first meeting – it all feels quite familiar.

My virtual chat with Julie feels a bit like that. The conversation flows freely as we talk about her life, her plans and her business interests, which are far removed from my own, while also crossing over on some level.

I catch up with her from her home in Lewes on a dreary Saturday morning. Offering reflexology and crystal treatments from her therapy room which sits atop her garden, Julie often finds that she's as much a talking therapist as anything else with appointments giving her clients time to offload and share. While it must be wonderful to know your clients trust you enough and feel comfortable to open their hearts, I would imagine that it can prove to be quite stressful.

Now Julie has had a bit of a year – broken toes, a broken foot, a period of living in a garden shed while her house underwent work, having her daughter move into her property and reopening her business fully after the pandemic, she joined the Seed to Vase course in March 2021, and since then has worked to transform her garden space into an idyll of nature befitting of her therapy room and the principles of her treatments.

"You know, I have absolutely loved the course," she told me. "I decided to take it on as I am a hopeless gardener!"

"My grandmother was incredible – she could just take a seed and grow it. She was green-fingered. I, on the other hand, am just hopeless. I don't know what to plant or when to plant it, or how to keep it alive – or at least I didn't until I started working through the course that is!"

Inspired by her grandmother, Julie joined the Seed to Vase course with another aim – she wanted to learn enough to share her knowledge with her own grandchildren – such a beautiful idea, don't you think?

"My garden is made up of two lawns, with steps in the middle between them. On one side I dug in lots and lots of manure, and now it's really thriving, that'll be where I will plant my bulbs – however, my luck with compost hasn't always been that successful..."

The addition of a puppy German Shepherd Pointer to Julie's life caused an unexpected complication.

"He liked relieving himself on my Sweetpeas. That was the end for them and my compost – which turned into a bed of mushrooms. I had to pull them all up, sadly, but it's all part of the learning, isn't it?"

I'm always cautious when it comes to compost. When we take a new delivery of manure or compost at Field Gate we test it first. By throwing a few seeds in it to see how they fare, we know if the compost is usable or not – after all, we wouldn't want to pop an untested compost on our blooms and undo all our hard work!

So, where does Julie intend to take her new-found skills?

"I am looking for ways to expand my business, so I am considering where I can take this in terms of developing my own range of essential oils."

"I have a huge eucalyptus in the garden, so I could start there, but there's also mint, lavender and rose that I can use in my healing, so that's something I have always wanted to explore. However, I didn't do the course to make a living, I did it to create a pleasant environment as people headed up to my treatment room."

With such a busy life, it was great to hear that growing her own flowers helps her to de-stress.

"You know, I love being able to look out of the window and see the flowers and plants I've grown myself. It gives me such a sense of pride to look outside and think I grew that - I did it! I kept it alive."

"But I've also had so much enjoyment from the course itself," which is, of course, something I am so pleased to hear.

"It's been so enjoyable watching you as part of the course – you are always so welcoming and happy. It's been great to see the journey of the course, to see your confidence grow and to see how it's expanded – and I have to add, there's a lot more to flower growing than you would think."

Julie really isn't wrong – there are so many layers to it, but the joy of the Seed to Vase course is that it lets you take your growing to whatever stage you want – from east straight-into-the ground sowing to the more complex side of growing like caring for and pruning roses and other annuals.

The Seed to Vase course comes with continued access to course materials, which will help Julie get started again for a beautiful garden in the summer of 2022.

"I have learned an awful lot – I just need to put it in action ready for next year so the space will look beautiful, and I don't need to buy things."

"I'll also save myself a fortune by growing my own stems!"

Yes – she will, and she'll also have the absolute joy that she's experienced this year, watching her own flowers grow and seeing them bloom and flourish.

I am excited by just how far Julie has come since March 2021. We are speaking 8 months after the course first started and here she is planning, and creating and finding ways to make flowers help the lives of others whilst also finding pleasure and stress relief in the actual gardening herself. Sounds like a win win situation to me.

16

KAREN DAVIES-JAMES

> "You can't stay in your corner of the Forest waiting for others to come to you. You have to go to them sometimes."
>
> — WINNIE THE POOH

Flowers have been in Karen Davies-James' life for so many years. Having completed a professional floristry course back in 2010, her life since then has been focussed on flowers.

From working with Yan Skates (recent competitor on the Netflix Show, 'The Big Flower Fight)' to creating displays in the flagship John Lewis store on Oxford Street, in the last decade or so Karen has gained a mountain of experience – mostly powered by adrenalin.

"By the time I had finished my course, I'd decided that I didn't want to go into working in a shop. I wanted to work on displays for events, so I put my feelers out and had some wonderful opportunities."

"The events I did with Yan were just amazing," Karen, a native of Loughton in Essex, told me when we caught up. "I'd turn up to help out and he'd give me a task of something like building a Taj Mahal out of grass – something I'd never done before, and I just had to go with it and learn quickly. I was involved in some spectacular events; Indian weddings, private parties in the most magnificent venues, and what I liked about them was the fact that you had a cut-off point. You had to be done and dusted by an exact time, ready to move out and let the guests enjoy your work."

"The work at the franchise in John Lewis Oxford Street did give me the chance to work in a huge, busy environment."

Having started to build her confidence and her experience, Karen started to run workshops in her local area, teaching fellow flower lovers how to arrange their blooms. Realising she was spending lots of cash on foliage, she took to her allotment and started a cut flower patch.

Disaster struck when she broke her hand in 2018 – her work with flowers was paused for a year while she recovered, but that didn't stop her from being inspired.

For many years Karen has enjoyed trips to the 'Fleuramour' flower event in Belgium, organised by Fleur Creatif.

"It is a most superb event – it's so different to any flower event in the UK; a beautiful chateau and its gardens, as well as the chapel, moat, and bridges, are decorated with flowers by florists from all over Europe. If I don't get to go on this break, I'd absolutely have withdrawal systems!"

Back at it in 2019, Karen spent some time with an Essex-based flower farmer, watching how the seasons impacted growing and farming, her confidence grew, and she started planning to get back to her cutting patch – and then came lockdown.

"During the lockdown, my allotment was my saving grace," she told me. "I grew lots of fruit and veg and also started with flowers again, cutting them for my pleasure, and also giving some to my friends to enjoy."

In early 2021, a friend introduced Karen to the Cut Flower Collective community on Facebook. From there she headed to the Seed to Vase course and now, a year on she's fully back to growing her cut flower patch and is ready to take on the flower world again with demos booked, with her own blooms set to take centre stage.

"The course I did with you really reaffirmed what I've been doing. It's given me more confidence to just go for it – I actually know now that I can grow enough to supply flowers for myself, and that to me is just brilliant."

"Not everything has been successful this year, though. I lost 28 Dahlia plants to slugs and snails, which was devastating, and some things didn't grow at all – but that's all part of nature, isn't it?"

Karen is right – one of the biggest lessons I've learned during my time as a Flower Farmer is how to learn from failure. Some seeds will never germinate – they'll stay dormant forever. Very often things won't be ready when they should be, or the rain will flatten everything – you must learn how to go with it, how to adapt to it and how to be fleet of foot if you need to – something, judging by Karen's past, she has absolutely no problem with.

Having redesigned her growing patch this year, Karen now has much more space to grow more big, beautiful blooms like Dahlia and she has a firm plan for 2022 - but and now she's worrying she will need more space!

"My allotment is about 120 feet long – half of it is given over the fruit and veg, and the other half is devoted to flowers – but I am worried I'll need more space!"

The theme of Karen's demonstrations is British flowers and encouraging people to grow their own by sharing her own experiences.

"I am completely convinced that British flowers are the way forward – and I want to spread the word."

From my own experience, I absolutely couldn't agree more. Over the last year or so I have seen a massive rise in people wanting to become flower farmers and people specifying that they want British-grown flowers. As the news gets around that most shop-bought flowers are flown in from thousands of miles away, people are keener to make a more sustainable choice – and that's exactly what I want to achieve with all this.

So, where does Karen see her flower journey heading?

"I'm not sure if this will be a hobby or business yet," she tells me. "I just have so much to learn."

"For example, I find that my flowers aren't lasting long after I've cut them – sometimes they've wilted before I've even got them home and I don't know what to do about that."

Luckily for Karen, I can help her with this – and this tip might be handy for you. If your fresh-cut flowers are looking as though they have wilted, they can be resuscitated!

Simply cut the stems at an angle and pop them into some fresh water and within 24 hours they will be rehydrated and beautiful again. Also, cutting them first thing in the morning is best- if you're cutting them in the day or even the evening, they won't have taken in enough water and so will wilt quickly.

Another tip that you might find handy is keeping your buckets are always completely clean. I bleach and sterilise mine regularly and ensure that I have a multitude of sizes available – after all, a Sweet Pea and a long-stemmed Roses can't really share a bucket for travel.

I adore the thought of Karen's plan. Spreading the word of growing your own seasonal cut flowers is just so incredible, and I can't wait to see how many people she inspires.

17

KIM VAUX

 "Rivers know this: There is no hurry. We shall get there someday."

— WINNIE THE POOH

Even after more than a decade as a flower farmer, I still have so much to learn. In fact, I am acutely aware that I'll never know everything there is to know about all things horticultural — and I'm okay with that.

Kim Vaux, one of my Seed to Vase community, feels the same. Having had a keen interest in flowers for many years, she joined the course after coming across an ad on social media.

Already experienced in working with flowers, the mum of two came to the course with the much-valued skill of floristry already under her belt, as she explained when she chatted to me from her home.

"I'd taken a few courses over the years, so when my daughter told us she was getting married in 2018, we decided that it would be lovely if I did some of the flowers for the celebrations."

"I ended up doing all the table centrepieces - partly to save money and partly to add a really personal touch. The arrangements I put together we as good as anything the florist had done – even if I do say so myself, so I did begin to wonder what else I could do with the skills I'd developed."

Having moved to Somerset from the South East in 2019 to be closer to her parents in Wales, the lack of available flowers during the pandemic gave her the impetus to grow her own, as she continued.

"Our new house in Somerset came with some land. We have a field for our two rescue ponies and then an orchard, which has lots of room to grow plants and flowers, so it was all perfect timing really."

"That said – the ponies are so fat! My daughter, who's an equine vet, keeps telling me off!"

With a handy husband and truckloads of her own, good quality pony manure on hand, Kim set about growing and learning, immersing herself in the course.

Already with some growing knowledge under her belt thanks to the beautiful orchard behind her house, which produces a wide selection of British apples each year, and her husband's green fingers, Kim has now truly been bitten by the flower-growing bug.

"My husband grows veg and he just loves a project, so he built me some raised beds. We'd already started growing flowers before the course started, but my knowledge just grew so much – I am learning something new every day!"

As the weeks went by and her garden grew, Kim realised that she was regaining some valuable 'me time', time for her to be alone with her thoughts, to enjoy the peace and the relish in her growing. Having lost her mother in early 2021, she discovered the community and the course provided her with a welcome distraction.

"Sadly, my mother died just before the course started," she told me. "I hadn't been able to see her for almost six months due to lockdowns.

"In the years before her passing both she and my father had suffered bouts of ill health. I'd spent a long period travelling between our house in the South East and South Wales to care for them, and that was hard - that's part of the reason we moved to the South West – now we are just a short drive from Wales."

"I find that I can really lose myself in the garden – it's so wonderful for my mental wellbeing and I feel very lucky to be able to get out there as much as I do!"

During the eight months of the course, Kim has seen some wonderful successes with what she has grown. She's started selling her blooms locally and has already been able to recoup almost half of her outlay so far.

"My husband is a retired Chartered Accountant, so he kept a spreadsheet of what we spent and what came in. I was surprised to see how much we'd managed to recoup, but I'm not doing this for profit – as long as I can cover the cost of my materials and keep my hobby going, I'll be happy!"

For Kim to have already covered fifty percent of her initial outlay in her first few months is very impressive – I would usually advise people not to expect to be in that position for a long while. Of course, it absolutely does help that Kim has her own manure factory – that will be a huge cost-saving, but I am always keen to impress that growing and selling flowers isn't an easy business – and it's certainly not the skipping-through-the-daisies lifestyle people might think. It's hard work, but it really does bring so much joy!

"I started selling the flowers in a little jar for a small amount – people seemed to like them, so I was keen to explore what else I could do."

"Towards the end of the summer I was selling bouquets from the local Post Office and the village store, and they were also very popular – they sold out most days, which was delightful to see."

Now completely hooked on growing, Kim has no plans to set up a big business with her newly found green fingers, but she still plans to sell her beautiful flowers during next spring and summer – but it strikes me that Kim isn't the type to limit herself!

"Well, I will definitely be producing and working with dried flowers more – I have a bit of a bug for them – they just look fabulous! I am also hoping to run some courses. Currently, I am working on a wreath-making course within the village – I'm keen to see how that goes and go from there."

"But, no – I have no desire to turn this into a business – I do not have the energy for that!"

"Between the dogs, the ponies, and the garden I am pretty busy," she said. "I don't have a lot of time for much else!"

With her tulips already planted, her Dahlias tucked up for the winter, and some new roses on the way, Kim has everything lined up for a gorgeous 2022. Thankfully, she's signed up to the *Best Bunch* group, so I can follow her journey and enjoy her growing with her.

"I had to sign up – I enjoyed the Seed to Vase course so much, and I also enjoyed the community that came with it – everyone is just so helpful and kind."

The community side of what we do here is so important to me – as I have already mentioned. Giving people time, space, and company to immerse themselves in something that completely takes them away from the pressures of everyday life – whether that's work, family, or health problems. I also think it's always wonderful to keep learning. I am continually learning new things – even after ten years of running the business I am still finding new plants and new techniques – and that's probably the part I love most about it all – and something lovely Kim has discovered too!

"Yes - this has all been a huge learning curve – I have absorbed an awful lot of new information, but I feel it's impossible to ever have the full knowledge of everything!"

18

LEANNE FISHWICK

"Any day spent with you is my favourite day. So, today is my
new favourite day."
Winnie the Pooh

We've all lived and breathed the pandemic over the last two
years, but for many of us, when the chatter and the news
became too much it was easy to turn off the TV or change the
channel and step away from it -even briefly.

However, Leanne Fishwick is still living and breathing it every
day – and she will be for a long time yet. You see, Leanne is a
Deputy Director of Operations for the NHS. That's right – she
has been immersed in the ins and outs of the whole pandemic
since day one – well, before what was day one for most of us.

I caught up with Leanne just as she finished a meeting about
the Omicron variant. A busy mum of two, she lives near St.
Albans with her husband and hectic schedule. When she's not
in work you can find her running around after the children, at
the gym, playing netball or, you guessed it, in her garden.

"I really value my downtime," Leanne tells me from her desk. "I've spent so much more time in the garden over the last year or so and it's really helped me to manage the stress and pressure of the hardest period of my twenty-year career."

Over the last few years, she's grown vegetables, and having been gifted an unwanted greenhouse by a friend, she decided she wanted to try something else, something new.

"My husband and I talked about me doing the course. Honestly, I wasn't sure, but he is amazing, and he encouraged me. He reminded me that lockdown meant that I had plenty of time on my hands when I wasn't at work and that I might not get this chance again."

Leanne started her cut flower journey with one of my online short courses - she immediately got the bug and signed up for the Seed to Vase course.

"I have tinkered with flowers here and there, but I've always mostly grown vegetables. I've bought bedding plants and

Cosmos and really enjoy flowers in the garden, but I never cut them – I've never felt like there's enough."

Discovering the joys of a cutting patch has been a revelation to Leanne. I can just picture it – after a hard day's work, spending time with her gorgeous plants, tucked away in the greenhouse, away from everyone (nobody bothers her there because the WiFi isn't great!), taking a breath and switching off.

"I've always grown vegetables, but next year I will be swapping the veg beds for flower beds -I can buy carrots cheaply enough, but I've come to realise that I can't buy flowers like the ones I grew this year – the Dahlias were just stunning."

Leanne's outlook is the same as mine. Whatever the debate around how supermarkets pay farmers, it's true; you can buy a bag of carrots for less than fifty pence, but you can't buy flowers cheaply.

The last year or two has seen the cost of flowers increase by almost forty percent due to a new import tax that came in with the UK leaving the European Union. The cost of imported stems is becoming prohibitive, so growing your own really is the way forward if you want to enjoy beautiful flowers in your home without paying through the nose.

"I fell in love with Dahlias," Leanne continued. "I'd never grown them before this year, but as soon as David Gillam's session was over, I went online and bought as many tubers as I could find!"

"My family thinks I am a crazy plant lady, no question!"

This is something I have heard from so many cut-flower-converts. It becomes addictive so quickly, and yes – you do find yourself talking to them!

"At the start of the course, the inside of my house just looked ridiculous. I wanted to give everything a go so there were seedlings everywhere!"

"I grew Dahlia, Cosmos, Snap Dragon, Cornflowers, Larkspur, Sweet Peas... so many beautiful flowers and things I hadn't seen before! I've had flowers for months now – the Sweet Peas were still going in November!"

That is a real joy when you grow your own flowers. There are only really two months of the year where you won't be able to cut flowers – probably January and February. If you really want to, you can force flowers but that's not something I'd recommend for hobbyists – and besides, enjoying fresh cut flowers ten months of the year is lovely.

"I was amazed that I was still able to use flowers from the garden at a dinner party I held in late November," Leanne added. "All of my friends were so impressed!"

"In fact, the cut flower patch has brought so many new conversations into my life – each flower is a talking point and I love chatting about the different varieties to visitors when they come to join me in the garden."

One of the greatest things for me is seeing the joy on people's faces when they see just how beautiful fresh cut flowers can be and how wonderful some of the varieties, we grow across the seasons here in the UK are - natural, beautiful, and as I have said so many times- just bursting with the most divine scent.

"I've really enjoyed giving other people flowers," Leanne agrees. "It's just so special – and I love it when I see their face and they see something new like a full bloom Snap Dragon."

So, what's the plan for the year ahead for Leanne?

"Well, I've already planted sixty tulip bulbs in beds ready for spring – although, I have decided I hate planting bulbs – probably because it's cold! However, the veg beds will be going, and I'll be growing more flowers!"

"Mainly over the next year, I really just want to spend as much time as I can in the garden. Being in the garden has been amazing for me – I can't think about anything else, and I just focus on what I need to do. It's wonderful!"

19

LESLEY BOAST

> "It isn't much good having anything exciting, if you can't share it with somebody."
>
> — WINNIE THE POOH

Talking to any of our health and care worker heroes fills me with just so much pride – especially when I think about how they have chosen to spend their precious 'downtime' with me and my team.

Lesley Boast is one of those heroes. She lives in Kent, working as a breast care nurse for Macmillan. In her spare time, she's also working as a nurse for the vaccination drive, and I caught up with her after a day spent giving small children their flu vaccination.

Like for all NHS workers, it's been a tough two years, but, in Lesley's wonderfully optimistic way she reminds me, "Still, at least there's flowers"

She's always adored gardening, something her parents encouraged her and her sister to enjoy from a young age when they were both given their own small bed to grow plants. Time spent with her Nan also gave her an education with growing, with Lesley spending hours tending to plants in her Nan's garden and learning their names.

Flowers have always had a huge role in Lesley's life, she recalls "Each spring we go to the local orchard, to pick daffodils whilst the lambs play in the fields around us, it reminds me of planting daffodil bulbs with my dad at the local hospice in memory of my mum. Flowers always remind me so much of different people in my life and their influence and guidance with appreciation."

When she married, the theme continued as her late mother-in-law and late husband also shared a passion for growing and now, today, Lesley finds herself with a large garden and an allotment where she spends most of her time growing flowers and vegetables.

"During the lockdown, I was still working but I needed something else to keep me busy. A friend of mine told me about The Cut Flower Collective and now, well, I'm just addicted!"

"I just cannot believe how many flowers I've grown this year," she continues. "There were so many days when I'd pick armfuls of flowers from the allotment – just so many; I couldn't believe it."

"It was such a pleasure to be able to share them with everyone. I've given away so many and it was wonderful to take them to church and decorate the building with them – just such a joy."

"I remember there was one day when everything was in bloom, and it felt like heaven."

I love this – I love the fact that even after years of growing Lesley is learning new things all the time and still being amazed by flowers and growing. For me, every year is a learning year. Right now, I am learning how to force flowers because we have an early spring wedding, and we need some hyacinths. It's like a big experiment – it's brilliant! There's always something to learn.

"You know, I would recommend the course to everyone - it's been so good," Lesley added. "It was a lovely community to be a part of – it felt like family, and everyone was so helpful."

"It's really made me think – I didn't know how much I was capable of," Lesley added.

Some of the plants that Lesley
had the most success with were the annuals, which are the most
pleasurable to grow as there's no long game.

"My Cosmos were dazzling – and the Nigella flowers were just
beautiful, but for me, the Ranunculi were just so pretty – I
couldn't believe how gorgeous they were."

So, what are Lesley's plans for 2022?

"Well, I've been doing some online floristry course, which has
been lovely, so I am hoping to grow more and sell some flowers
to raise funds for the church. I would also like to run some
classes, like the wreath-making course I ran at the church this
winter."

20

LISA HURLEY

 "It never hurts to keep looking for sunshine"

— EEYORE

This chapter is dedicated to Lisa's Mother who passed away in late 2021. Lisa recalls the lovely times they spent talking about the Seed To Vase course and she will always hold these memories close to her heart. Lisa's Mother inspired her to start growing cut flowers and she hopes that her she will do her proud in the years to come.

I caught up with Lisa as she was recovering from Coronavirus. She was feeling better, but it had been a tough week or so for her and her husband, who was also poorly.

"Thankfully, I didn't have it as bad as some people have had it, but a couple of days in bed have given me plenty of time to do some planning for next year!" she tells me from her home.

Such a lovely, gentle lady, she's recently found herself as an empty nester with her son moved out and daughter living at university. So now, after many years, Lisa and her husband are home alone – and it's all very new!

Home is a pretty five-acre farm near Long Marsden. Its occupants include bees, chickens, a dog and a cat, along with a healthy vegetable garden that Lisa has tended to for many seasons.

With a desire to take the next step, after planting bulbs and seeds into the flower beds at the rear of the house and finding the blooms to be thriving, a sign-up to the Seed to Vase course followed - and since then, she hasn't looked back.

"For my 50th birthday I asked for a polytunnel," not your usual gift for a milestone birthday but, yes - I get it.

"It's really large – twenty feet by ten, and it's in an area of the farm we've fenced off specifically for flowers," she added. "We get a lot of deer here and the rabbits are a pest, so we had to fence the area off, otherwise I'd never manage to grow anything!"

During our chat, Lisa shares with me her struggles with anxiety. She's experienced anxiety symptoms for many years but it was her own investigations that led her to realise that she was experiencing the very early stages of menopause and that it was that that was causing the continual anxiety.

It's only in the last couple of years that it's been recognised that for many years women have been misdiagnosed with anxiety and depression when in fact their symptoms were caused by menopause and could be treated with HRT or other therapies. Recently, the volume has been dialled up on the conversation around menopause thanks to campaigners such as Davina McCall and MP Carolyn Harris, who have demanded an end to what they call 'medical sexism' – and it's working. Thankfully! Now minds are opening to the impact of 'the change' – and I am so glad to see it.

For Lisa, growing, and cutting has helped her to cope with the symptoms and feelings of anxiety – but not in the way you might expect.

Lisa also struggled when her mother was diagnosed with a terminal illness. They shared a common love of gardening and Lisa's mother was her greatest champion. These memories of the time they shared discussing the course will live on in Lisa forever.

"I found that I had far too many flowers for us to have at home – even though I have them everywhere, so I popped a message upon the village Facebook page advertising little bunches of flowers in pretty pink jars."

"I charged between £10 and £15 per jar of flowers – not intending to make a profit, but with the aim of spending whatever money that they made on more bulbs for next season."

"I was so excited that they went down well – I've even had people come back for second orders, which is helping to grow my confidence – but before I posted them for sale, I was filled with anxiety."

"What if they die before I get them to people? What if people don't like them? So many what-ifs – but in the end, I needn't have worried."

For Lisa, there are no plans to go big with her business-although I must share, she has the potential to do something with it. The land she has at home is the same space as I have here at the farm – five acres – that's plenty to make a good living out of flowers – and, as she already has the infrastructure in place to grow en-masse. She's also had a golden taster year – she really is ready to go!

Her little business has also had lots of interest from florists – something I could have only dreamed of when I started.

"When I was ill with Covid-19, I received a message from a local florist. She's only been in business a shirt time and asked me if I might be able to work with her to supply British flowers."

"I was so excited and surprised – and so grateful!"

How incredible is that? It's fair to say that high street florists have been more open to buying British fresh cut flowers in recent months for sustainability and monetary reasons, but this is the first time I've heard of a florist reaching out directly. That said – I can see why! It seems like Lisa has a bit of a natural flair when it comes to all things social media. Her Instagram grid is gorgeous – and she already has almost 1500 followers (at the time of writing).

"I love creating and posting on Instagram," she added. "It's something I enjoy and can get my teeth into."

This is great – for many businesses, Instagram is just an irritating 'nice to have' – they underestimate the power and the reach it has, especially when the content is 'on-brand', but it really can't be underestimated. Trust me, I wouldn't spend a minimum of two hours a day, every day, creating content for it if it wasn't valuable to Field Gate Flowers.

So, how does 2022 look for Lisa now that Petal Patch is on its feet?

"I have learned a lot this year – if it wasn't for the course, I would have really struggled with getting going, but it kept me motivated and the results were just so rewarding, so I have high hopes for next year."

I am a firm believer in fate, and I really believe that flowers have found their way to Lisa for a reason. She's had her children and they have flown the nest – it's now time for her to do something just for her, to live and grow – and get her confidence back.

The motto I try and live by is that whatever happens, I will find a way through it. It does take a couple of times of realising that you can find a way to have confidence in that mantra, but it's so true – there's always a way to fix a problem – but sometimes, you just need to have the bravado to *fake it 'til you make it*, but I am sure Lisa has it in her – and she has all of those beautiful flowers tucked up and ready to grow to give her that hope.

"I am terrified!" Lisa agrees, "but I am going to adopt your mantra – I will find a way!"

Go bold, Lisa. You've got this.

21

RACHEL ARNOTT

 "You're braver than you believe, stronger than you seem, and smarter than you think."

— WINNIE THE POOH

One of the trickiest parts of moving into the flower farming industry for those who are completely new to it is often the floristry side of the business. Putting together beautiful floral displays is an art form; a skill that takes many years of work and practice to hone, but one that is so essential when it comes to doing justice to any type of flower.

The wonderful thing about Rachel is that she came to the Seed to Vase course directly from a career as a florist - a career journey that had enveloped almost half of her life. She already understood flowers and foliage and how to make them work to their best effect.

Hailing from Blackpool, Rachel was made redundant from her job at the start of the coronavirus pandemic however, as a new mum to a five-month-old son, she felt grateful for the extra time at home that lay ahead of her.

Like many others, an online advertisement led her to us, but for Rachel, it offered an opportunity that was something far more important than a hobby – it offered her the chance to start a new journey and to learn skills she'd always been interested in.

"Even though I had been a florist for all of my adult life, I guess I was ignorant to the facts about where the flowers came from," Rachel told me. "I never really thought about it – they just appeared in the shop to work with."

"I've always wanted to know more about growing my own flowers, and the course offered the perfect way for me to do that."

As a new mum, Rachel was also excited about the prospect of taking her little boy, Ethan, on the journey with her.

. . .

"In a time of screens and gaming, I always knew that I wanted Ethan to grow up outside and to learn that outside is better than being stuck inside."

"I had this vision of us working together, sitting, and planting seeds and digging, but the reality is very different!"

Together, in the small garden of their semi-detached home, Rachel and Ethan plant and grow beautiful seasonal British flowers following the steps and advice from the Seed to Vase course, but with a full-time job and a young son, Rachel isn't quite ready yet to leap into being a fulltime flower farmer just yet.

However, that doesn't mean that she doesn't harbour big plans.

"I have so many ideas around what I can do in this industry," Rachel continued as we chatted. "I want to teach people, I want to share the joy of flowers, of growing them and arranging them and I want to do that with as many people as I can."

"I'm just not quite ready yet to take that big leap."

At 8 months in length, the cut flower course that Rachel joined was quite the commitment – especially with a baby, and it's opened her eyes to a new lifestyle journey.

"I've really enjoyed the course – it has been just incredible. I must confess though that I did fall behind a little bit, but everything is still available, so I can work through it at my own pace."

It goes without saying, that as part of my crusade to have everyone in the UK growing their own flowers to cut, I am working on Rachel, encouraging her to bring her skills and passion to the industry – after all, she already understands the floristry side of the business – the side I'd consider to be the toughest half.

With access to a polytunnel and land, Rachel is fortunate enough to be able to make a strong start – I just need to persuade her – after all, what does she have to lose?

"I miss the floristry side of things and I want to get back to it."

"Being a florist is like giving someone a piece of yourself," says Rachel. "You put a piece of yourself in every bouquet and display that you create – it's like creating a piece of art."

Of course, as a florist using seasonal, British flowers, wherever Rachel's floristry journey takes her next will be very different from the last path she was on.

I encourage full sustainability on the whole flower farming journey. From ditching the awful foam flower oasis and not using any pesticides to only using seasonal blooms and wireframes, the whole purpose of the movement of the cut flowers is to reduce the impact of floristry and flower gifting on the planet. By reducing air miles and the impact on the earth from growing non-indigenous flowers in places like Africa to meet global demand for perfect, all-year-round bouquets if everyone grew their own flowers for cutting, we would save millions of tonnes of CO_2 each year and help biodiversity to thrive here in the UK.

"You know, I don't think I want to go back to the way I used to do floristry," Rachel added as we talked further.

"I don't want to go back to wrapping flowers in plastic and using imported flowers – I want to put the environment and sustainability to be at the forefront of everything I do however this works out."

Watching Rachel's journey so far has been brilliant, and I can't wait to see how she progresses. Her views on sustainability and the fact that she already has the talent and skills in terms of the floristry side of the business are just what the British flower industry needs right now, and I cannot wait to see what she does with her skills and resources.

What I also love about Rachel is that she's managed to start this journey from the back garden of her house, proving that you don't need swathes of land to get going. As she has proven – growing a small patch for your own enjoyment is achievable whatever space you have – and it brings so much joy!

I'll be following her closely and, as with all the Seed to Vase graduates, will be around if she needs any help or advice.

22

RACHEL COOPER

> "When you see someone putting on his Big Boots, you can be pretty sure that an Adventure is going to happen."
>
> — WINNIE THE POOH

Creative people really excite me - the energy, the ideas, their general vibe – it's just wonderful to be around, and I love that I meet so many of them through the Cut Flower Collective.

One of these wonderful creatives is the darling Rachel Cooper who lives just outside Abergavenny in Monmouthshire, Wales.

Having moved down the valley a little from Brecon, Rachel and her husband Ian live in a rented cottage which is surrounded by rolling Welsh hills and breath-taking scenery. Their life, although busy and exciting is incredibly fulfilling although, I must admit, I don't know how she does it all!

Amongst her interests, Rachel tells me that she loves music, baking, socialising, reading, cooking, singing in a local choir, and working with Ian to keep their several Ukulele groups going! As if that wasn't enough, between them they have four grown-up children aged between 19 and 27 and a two-year-old grandson to boot.

Until February 2020, Rachel was a Library Assistant at Brecon Library, a job she completely adored, but one that lost its shine due to cutbacks and the closing and relocating of the library. She started to think about what she really wanted to do, about what she was passionate about, and about what she wanted to do with her time.

She took the leap, and once she'd left her job, Rachel took a job in a local café – and then Covid hit. Being laid-off followed meant one thing – more time in the garden!

"I have always loved flowers and enjoyed gardening," Rachel tells me when we catch up from her home. "I love the wildlife, cottagey kind of garden – that pretty, rustic feel."

Rachel's flower-growing journey had started a little before we crossed paths. Perennials were always growing in her garden and in the spring of 2019, inspired by a friend, she added some annuals to her garden. Having enjoyed the annuals Rachel planned to grow more in 2020 – which of course, she had plenty of time for – as did we all!

I caught up with Rachel after a day's trading at the popular Abergavenny Market. With the last of her flowers in tow (it was the start of December when we spoke), some gorgeous crafts, and some dried bits, she'd had a successful day and I can really see the start of something wonderful in what she's doing.

Meadow Garden Cottage Flowers is the name of her business – and it seems that its pure aim is to bring joy through flowers and gorgeous things. The ethos of the business lies firmly in sustainability with Rachel ensuring that all her wrapping and trimmings are completely planet-friendly – something I very much approve of!

"I have learned so much over the last year," she shares. "And I am sure there's still so much more to learn ."

"The pure joy of growing flowers to give, to bring into the home, to sit amongst and look at them, while helping wildlife is absolutely what I am passionate about. I also care deeply about the wellbeing aspect of it all and would love to understand more about that."

That is indeed the joy of growing and sharing flowers. There's nothing that's quite as special as sharing a bouquet of flowers that you have picked and grown yourself. So much love and time are invested in them and that really does shine through.

"I have felt for a long time how nice it would be to pick your own flowers for somebody's birthday or other occasions, rather than buy them from a supermarket," Rachel adds. "I really want to look into how I can expand that by sending flowers."

As well as her fledgling business, Rachel is also a part-time gardener. Having completed a WRAG Scheme (Work and Retrain as a Gardener) course, she has a wealth of skills and knowledge that have allowed her to take on several private clients as well as have the privilege of tending to a two-acre walled garden.

"The walled garden is an absolute joy to work in," Rachel tells me. "This year I have been involved with helping in the expansion of the cut flower part of the garden, and it's given me so much inspiration - it leaves me feeling incredibly energised."

The WRAG Scheme is just brilliant – I currently have a gardener working for me who is training under this scheme. It's a wonderful way to retrain in later life and to create a new career. So many people are doing it after years and decades of working in offices or indoor environments. It's probably another outcome of the pandemic, but I am seeing more people change careers and move into more physical, outdoor jobs and that's just brilliant!

"The main motivation for me when I left my job at the library after 19 years was to take back control of my life – it was a scary thing to do after almost two decades of structure and stability, but I'm lucky – I have Ian and he supported and encouraged me, having been a freelance Musician and Teacher for over 25 years and I am so glad I went for it!"

"It's funny how things happen, isn't it? You just put things out there and fate can take over!"

I am a huge believer in serendipity, and I think Rachel's story is a testament to that. She was clearly always meant to be on this path.

"All that said, my WRAG training was complimented by the Seed to Vase course, it really helped me focus my mind and it gave me a structure, a purpose and a goal, and everyone was just so wonderful. I feel like the cohort is a little family."

So – what's on the agenda for 2022?

"I am constantly having ideas about what I want to do and the things I could do," Rachel tells me. "I want to do workshops and perhaps even start a flower subscription – and of course, I will do more markets because they're brilliant. They give me the chance to have conversations with so many like-minded people and to share my flowers and plants – and I love that!"

"Gardening and flowers are just so good for the soul, and I want to share that with as many people as I can."

I am excited to follow Rachel's journey, to see her confidence grow, and to see how she grows and develops as a gardener and florist. If she just takes a step back, reflects, and enjoys I know she will realise her worth and just how much magic her talent and passion can bring to the world.

23

RACHEL MORTISHIRE SMITH

> "We didn't realise we were making memories; we just knew we were having fun."
>
> — WINNIE THE POOH

Wow! If you ever need any motivation or inspiration to keep on keeping on, then this chapter is for you!

Rachel Mortishire-Smith is an ex-primary school teacher from Macclesfield. She lives in a beautiful house called the Homestead, inside a park with her husband and has no fewer than four jobs!

She's a tutor, she works in the local museum, a church children's worker and in less than a year, she has built up a wonderful little flower business - all this with just one hand! You see, in December 2020 Rachel had a nasty accident that left her needing a joint replacement in her finger. Throughout 2021 she had four operations on her finger and completed lots of the course with just one hand!

Amazing, right?

"At the start of the course I was in lots of pain – and to add to it, my knees are giving out too – I am far too young for all this!" Rachel jokes when we caught up. It had been quite to effort to pin her down for a chat - as you can probably imagine – but we managed to squeeze fifteen minutes in as she prepared for the three pre-Christmas wreath-making courses she's hosting in a local apple barn.

Having always been a gardener, this year she has really elevated her growing. Supported by her wonderful father and husband who have lent a hand when she's needed it (sorry, couldn't resist!), she has grown in ten newly installed beds and boxes over the last year and has experienced the real joy that comes from growing from seeds and bulbs.

Luckily, her husband's lockdown hobby was woodwork and so he's building beds for her "by the minute" meaning that there really is no end to Rachel's growing potential – especially now she's discovered the joy of growing from seed herself.

"Before the Seed to Vase course, I had never grown anything from seed. I've always bought plants and stuck them in the ground with no real idea of what I was doing – I definitely killed more than a few things, but I am all for growing from seed now – it's just so exciting."

She's right – it might seem like a small thing, but when you see those tiny seeds first start to propagate and you realise that something you're growing is coming to life it really is incredibly exciting! When you're in nature the smallest things make you so excited; things you wouldn't have given a second glance were you not gardening and experiencing the unique love and joy that growing your own brings. It's much more of an emotional investment than a time investment.

Of course, Rachel's journey involved lots of hiccups – something which is absolutely to be expected, but as I've said so many times, every day in the garden is a learning day!

"At the start of the course I really struggled to believe that the things I was planting out would come to anything, but I listened to all of the advice from the course and kept the faith and somehow it happened, and it was wonderful!"

Rachel also managed to find some peace and rest amidst her busy life thanks to her garden.

"It (the garden) became a wonderful place to sit and watch the hens and listen to the birds -especially in the early morning and dusk watering times."

The core ethos of Rachel's business – HOMEstead GROWN – is about using the things that we have naturally available to us to bring flowers into the home. I adore this notion and wish I could be as dedicated to this way of doing things as Rachel is.

"I am foraging and growing everything that I use," she tells me. "I don't want to buy in anything apart from seeds and bulbs, and I'm lucky I can access so much of what I need due to where I live and the friends I have."

"Everything I use is local and sourced by me. All the moss I am using in the wreath-making workshops I have taken from our lawn. Last year that moss was the bane of my life, now it's the most wonderful thing! I also forage at a local farm, and the park keepers and friends who are tree surgeons lob lovely branches and bits of wood over the fence for me – it all gets used!"

So, now Rachel has been bitten by the British flower bug, what's next?

"Well, I've managed to set up a small business," she tells me. "I didn't set out to do that – it just sort of found me. People were coming across my work on Instagram, and they started asking me if they could buy it."

"That said, I'm so busy now I couldn't take on anything else – it's just non-stop!"

Rather impressively, Rachel's wreath-making workshops, 'Found and Foraged' will be delivered to 45 people across three sessions – and there's scope for more! That's no mean feat – especially as she's not done any paid advertising!

"It's all come from social media," she continues. "which is just amazing!"

Agreed! All the business she has secured is organic and has been achieved purely through her wonderful work and the flowers speaking for themselves – how brilliant?

Thanks to her handy husband, Rachel is set to have her own workshop in their garage and plans to sell from her home – with its fortunate location in a well-used park, she's sure to do brilliantly.

"I just need to plan," Rachel tells me. "Making sure I have what I need when I need it takes planning – but I am getting there. My bulbs are in for next year and seeds are sown, so I am already ahead for 2022."

It does take two or three years to get the planning down to a tee, but Rachel will get there, and when she does, I am quite convinced that she will need to take on a whole team to support her because what she's doing is clearly something wonderful that's really struck a chord locally. Her environmental ethos is idyllic and is exactly what we need to see more of across the whole of the UK flower industry.

HOMEstead GROWN is one to watch for sure!

24

SARAH MCCUBBINE

> " "As soon as I saw you, I knew an adventure was going to happen."
>
> — WINNIE THE POOH

The more I talk to people (and I do that a lot), the more I realise what a fundamental impact the pandemic has had on lives. I know that might sound like an obvious thing to say, so let me explain further.

Pre-pandemic, we all went about life doing what we did because that's what we did. Nothing was questioned. We went to work, we got stuck in traffic, we came home and did what we needed to. It didn't really matter whether we liked the jobs we had or not – that's just how it was – we didn't know there was an alternative.

Then the lockdown came and with it came an enforced stop for some, and for others an enforced ramping up. For many, it brought with it the idea of working from home – or not working at all. It brought a different pace of life – and that forced many people to think again.

Sarah McCubbine lives in a little village just outside London. The wife of a cattle farmer and mum of three, pre-pandemic she was a Forest School teacher, working with children aged 5-7, outside the classroom environment, exploring nature and developing confidence through hands-on experiences in a natural setting.

When the pandemic hit, she was unable to work, so instead, she had what she describes as the 'best summer ever'.

"I have always loved gardening," she tells me. "My Mum was a gardener and I have really vivid memories of being about five or six and my Dad teaching me how to sow Collius, Lupin, and other flowers correctly, so I spent the summer growing."

"I know I shouldn't say that it was a wonderful summer because it was tough for so many people, but for me, it was fabulous!"

While planning the flowers for her daughter's wedding, Sarah came across the Cut Flower Collective on Facebook. From there everything just snowballed – she found herself signing up to courses on growing, sowing, and cutting everywhere – even an RHS course in the childhood back garden of Anne Boleyn at the magnificent Hever Castle. What a journey!

Sarah's love of gardening and flowers landed her with the gig of creating the floral displays for her daughter's wedding, which was also hit by restrictions and the pandemic.

The plan was to grow wildflowers to create whimsical, romantic displays of seasonal blooms. Having seconded a field at the family farm, she created a one-acre wildflower meadow, which from her pictures looks magical – but British weather being what it is, things didn't quite go as intended.

"The wedding was initially in the diary for May 2020, but it was pushed back two or three times and we eventually we set on a date in July 2021."

"However, the weather in the week before the wedding was just hideous – I was looking back at my phone's camera roll and found a picture of my beautiful flower meadow all flattened and beaten down by the rain the week before the wedding."

"I have so many pictures of flattened Oxeye Daisies!"

It all worked out, however, and now, with her other daughters marrying next year, Sarah finds herself planning and growing ready to tackle the challenges they will bring.

But it's not going to stop there for Sarah.

Thanks to a small inheritance, Sarah was able to give up her job, and now it's her intention to make flower farming her career. With other weddings already booked in for next summer, and with some interest in terms of wholesale from local florists, 2022 looks set to be a good year for the soon-to-be established Smallfield Flower Farm.

"When I set out on this journey, I had no intention of making this my living," she tells me. "But, I had so many compliments about the flowers I was growing, I felt that I needed to give it a go.".

While the job of living on and being part of a working farm is hard, to say the least, Sarah finds herself in the fortunate position of having access to many of the tools and machinery that really pile on the costs when it comes to setting up in business.

With an acre of the farm now dedicated to growing, polytunnels in the offing, and all the manure any grower could dream of, Sarah's journey has started – but although she has everything she needs, that doesn't mean it's going to be easy!

"I need to prove to my husband that I can make a go of it – and I am determined to!"

"The land that we have turned over to the flower farm is now no longer in production for growing grass or grazing cattle, so I need to make this work – we are diversifying a small part of the farm, so it has to pay."

I sit on a board of a group of more than 1000 farmers, and I know that making money from farming is hard – just as it is difficult to make money from farming flowers. I often encounter the opinion that farming flowers and not cereal or livestock isn't 'real' farming, and often face the argument that it's horticulture, not agriculture. It goes without saying, I am firmly in the agriculture camp on this one – and often, farmers are astounded about how the turnover of a flower farm is different from that of a traditional British farm.

"I have to prove him right," Sarah continues. "I just want to prove it's more than just playing."

I am sure that Sarah will prove the worth of her endeavours – I think she's done it the right way also. She's spent the year getting all her ducks in a row, learning from her mistakes, planning her beds, and building her confidence – which really is the key when it comes to setting up your own business.

"I suffer from terrible imposter syndrome. I hadn't heard the phrase before I started the course with you, but I think I have suffered from it my whole life."

"For example, in my previous job, I never had less than a 'good' or 'outstanding' rating my work, yet I always thought I was rubbish at it. I have always been the same with flowers, always pointing out my mistakes but not looking at my successes."

"As part of working with you I have had to look back at the pictures I have taken and when I did and saw of some of the arrangements I've made, I thought 'you know – they're pretty good' – I just need to keep growing my confidence – which is probably the biggest learning curve I have been on over the last year."

"I just can't believe how quickly the year has gone and how much I have grown since I began the course."

By now, you'll know that I love hearing things like this from course attendees, but I always want to know how the course has helped them to grow in their knowledge and skills.

"Aside from growing my confidence, one of the biggest things I have learned is about timing."

"I got terribly excited and planted all of my seedlings without having a plan as to where I was going to put them. I also learned that I need to plan my beds – I didn't do that this year and ended up moving things around, which isn't a wise idea!"

We all make mistakes – it's how we learn. Even after ten years we still make mistakes – but we are also still learning – and that's important too!

"Next year will be better," she reassures herself.

One of the next steps for Sarah will be to learn to understand the dark arts of setting up the business to run and work as a business – thinking about tax, profit, and loss, and pricing really isn't the most exciting things when you like being out in the fresh air planting and pruning but to make a success of Small-field Flower Farm, it needs to be done.

"Yes – that's the next stage - I don't know where to start, but it's top of the list!"

I am looking forward to seeing how Sarah's journey progresses. I'm particularly intrigued to see how she will deal with the challenges many of the other fledging flower farmers don't have – I am sure she can do it, though!

25

SHARAYNA DESOUZA

 "It never hurts to keep looking for sunshine."

— EEYORE

This book features the stories of plenty of gardeners who have access to large gardens, allotments, and even farms, but this chapter is all about achieving joy from growing in an altogether different space.

Sharayna Desouza lives in Brentford, West London. Hailing from Mumbai, she and her partner live in an apartment block in a built-up area – but this is no ordinary apartment block - it's an apartment block with a difference. You see, the roof of the apartment block houses a raised bed allotment for residents, where they can grow fruit, veg and, of course, flowers – a fabulous idea to help us regreen our cities, help the planet out and help people live more sustainably.

Sharayna and her partner took a lease of one of these spaces back in 2019 and proceeded to grow the staples; spuds, tomatoes, and a few extra treats such as aubergines – it was here her current journey started.

"I have always grown vegetables, and I have to say, I am pretty good at it," she told me when we caught up, having just harvested an aubergine – in November! Clearly, she's very good at all this!

Having discovered our courses in an allotment Facebook group, Sharayna entered one of my competitions, winning herself a space on the Seed to Vase course, which is where the flower-growing bug bit. And even though she has limited space, she's had some success – and is already planning and planting for next spring!

"I have my raised bed and I have taken charge of some tiny communal flower beds that border the roof allotment," she told me. "But I need more space!"

"This year I've tried growing some things in pots. I tried poppies, but I didn't have a lot of success, however, I am proud to say that I have managed to grow two Dahlias from seed in pots – they're beautiful."

"Oh – and I managed to get my Christmas cactus to flower, which is very exciting!"

Sharayna's energy is infectious – she so full of joy and excitement, but with a job as a compliance officer for a hedge fund in the city, her days can be incredibly exhausting – and pandemic aside, the last few years of her life have been incredibly stressful.

"At the start of 2019, I was made redundant from my job. My partner and I had just moved into this apartment and it was an incredibly worrying time – especially as I was in the UK on a visa that was sponsored by my workplace."

"During those darker days when I was looking for a new job, I would head to the roof, to my raised bed allotment every day and spend two or three hours weeding it and preparing it ready for planting."

"Even in the pouring rain and the cold of winter it made me feel great like I had a sense of purpose and something to get up for every day – it did so much for my mental health."

"Now, I am just completely addicted – I love growing and gardening. If you ever have a job vacancy come up – let me know!"

Like so many gardeners, Sharayna now heads straight to her outdoor space after work to check in on her plant babies, have a chat with them, and make sure they're watered and thriving.

"I work for a hedge fund in the West End – heading straight to the roof after work helps the stresses of the day just melt away," she continues. "Those fifteen minutes are an absolute lifesaver."

I totally get this! When I started the farm, I was still working in my corporate job. Every day I'd go home and potter in the garden, which I found so wonderful for de-stressing – planting seeds and bulbs while listening to music just made everything else seem so unimportant.

I could feel the strains of the day evaporate away and was able to get my mind to a place where I'd be able to think 'I've had enough of today – let's move on'.

I've said it more than once and I'll say it again - nature really is the best medicine. The sense of achievement from growing and transforming brings great joy and the fresh air and the great British weather are just so good for the soul.

Sharayna agreed, "Every day I'd see something new happen, and when the flowers were blooming, I was like 'oh my God! I have actually grown those!' I felt so proud!"

"You know, recently, I have been thinking that maybe I am in the wrong profession."

"Over the last year, I have had a few anxiety attacks and thought I couldn't do my job anymore," she continued. "Gardening helped me manage that, but there have been times I have just wanted to quit my job and become a gardener."

"So, if you have a vacancy, I'll quit my job tomorrow and come work for you!"

I love this spirit – and in fact, one of my horticulturists, Emma, followed a similar path to that that Sharayna is aspiring to, quitting a high-flying job, studying with the RHS, and then taking the leap. I do believe that becoming a farmer, a gardener or a florist is a vocation – you must be called to it – and maybe this is her calling.

So, what's next for Sharayna's journey?

"Next year, I want to grow more flowers – I am short on space, but I have taken possession of a big recycling tub. I've put it next to my raised bed, so I am going to plant that up with flowers for next year."

"I've also been given a rose plant recently, so I am excited to plant that up and see it in bloom next summer."

"But overall – I just want to keep having fun with it."

And that's the most important thing having fun with it. Buying a £2.99 packet of seeds and throwing them in the ground and seeing what happens is nothing - it's just fun and getting enjoyment from growing must be the most important thing.

"You know, this year has been a lot of fun," Sharayna finished. "I have enjoyed it, even though I feel like I am so bad at it, but everyone was so helpful, which has been amazing."

"And now, if you asked me what gives me the most joy and makes me happiest, I would straightaway say it's growing and gardening."

26

SUE MCGLASSON

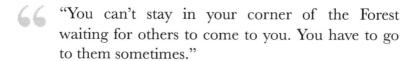

"You can't stay in your corner of the Forest waiting for others to come to you. You have to go to them sometimes."

— WINNIE THE POOH

For me, amidst all the angst and worry, one of the most special things about the Coronavirus lockdowns of 2020 is the fact that it created, for so many of us, an opportunity to fold back into the communities that surround us.

A smile and a chat on the daily walk, checking in on elderly neighbours, speaking to people you've seen around but never chatted to before, and pulling together to keep morale up were some of the most wonderful things about the lockdowns, and for many of us, they became so important and created enduring memories.

For one of our wonderful course attendees, Sue McGlasson from Guilsborough in Northamptonshire, it was one of these supportive check-ins that started her flower-growing journey.

"There's a lovely lady called Gay who lives behind me that I got to know really well during the pandemic," Sue says.

"Gay has large, landscaped gardens and she's always so busy in them. She set up our village gardening WhatsApp group and we got chatting about flowers - it was her that encouraged me to start a cut flower patch."

"So, yes- it's a cliché, but lockdown is to blame for my seed and flower addiction! I love it - seeing something grow from a seed into beautiful things: it blows my mind how actually this happens!"

So, after being bitten by the flower-growing bug, Sue, a mum to four teenagers, began researching, and through that, she came across the cut flower course.

"During my first year of growing things didn't go so well. I had seedlings all over the house and I didn't yield a lot of flowers, but I so enjoyed it."

"My husband thought I was mad!"

From here on in things began to take root for Sue (yes, pun intended), who now has her own allotment and several beds in her garden.

"Since I found the course online, I have learned so much," Sue continued.

"Now I am growing so many flowers and I have lots of plans to grow more. I've turned all my veg beds into flowers beds and I'm quickly running out of room."

"My husband has itchy feet, and he often mentions moving. Until now I have always said no, but perhaps it is now time to start looking for a house with a bigger garden so I can grow even more!"

As we know, the act of growing flowers and getting out in the fresh air has an incredible effect on bringing down those stress levels – and Sue is the first to acknowledge this. Her busy life as a working mum with a house full of teens and a self-employed husband is a huge amount to keep on top of but getting outside really gives Sue the space and time to clear her mind and think.

Her flower growing has brought her immense joy – and that much sought-after 'me' time.

Currently, Sue, and her friend who grows with her, have no plans to move into the commercial flower farming business. Instead, they find masses of joy in sharing their blossoms with friends, neighbours, and elderly residents in their village.

"People are always so pleased when we hand them a bunch of our cut flowers," Sue told me.

And why wouldn't they be?

The cut flower course shows you how to grow pesticide-free British seasonal flowers that smell incredible – unlike the mass-produced flowers, which are bred for purpose instead of pleasure. Not only does their scent bring joy, but they're beautiful too – especially some of the more dramatic blooms like Dahlias and in-season roses.

The course is also a real knowledge builder – as Sue found out - it has elevated her knowledge and growing experience, providing her with the confidence to expand her collection and to understand where and when things need to be planted and how to best look after them.

"The course provided me with so much information. I feel I understand enough to grow and develop what I'm doing, and while I have no plans to expand this into a business currently, I know that the time with Roz and her team has given me a map to help me take things forward if I want to."

"I learned about timings, successional sowing, and so much practical information. I'm also great at naming plants and flowers now – I couldn't do that before, but now I can recall plenty of names off the top of my head!"

Even now, I am always learning and making mistakes. Each year and each season bring with it new challenges to work with – this year there were spots we didn't rabbit-proof properly and plenty of things we didn't stake and support properly; something Sue is coming to understand.

"It's a real learning journey," she added. "I am picking up new information all the time."

"But I must admit, now the Seed the Vase course is over I will feel a little lost without the check-ins and the videos - obviously I still have access to the course material, but I will miss everyone and all of the support the groups and check-ins bring."

When I think about it, it's this return to nature that's one of the most valuable outcomes of the Coronavirus pandemic.

We've all begun returning to the earth, appreciating everything our country and communities have to offer, finding new communities and new ways of living.

For Sue, the supportive chats with her neighbour during the longest days of the pandemic have opened up a whole new world for her; one that she didn't ever feel she would get involved in, but one that's become a home to her.

She doesn't mind the slog of pushing wheelbarrows of water around or the hard work involved in changing up veg beds to flower beds – in fact, she finds it cathartic, and it's absolutely changed her life.

"You know, I don't think I will ever stop growing," Sue enthused – and for me, that's just the most wonderful thing to hear.

AFTERWORD

So that's a wrap as they say. I truly hope with all my heart that you will be inspired by the stories in this book. All participants on the course came together from different walks of life to form one engaged community. What they all had was a love of the outdoors and the enthusiasm to give it a go. I for one am immensely proud of every one of them.

And in the words of Christopher Robin

 "You're braver than you believe, stronger than you seem, and smarter than you think."

We would love you to join our community.

Here are the various ways you can do this.

WEB: www.fieldgateflowers.co.uk

FACEBOOK GROUP: The Cut Flower Collective

https://www.facebook.com/groups/768190817371225

Scan the QR code below:

INSTAGRAM: http://www.instagram.com/fieldgateflowers

ACKNOWLEDGEMENTS

Of course, no book is complete without acknowledgments. No man is an island, and I could not have written this book without the help of the following: -

Abi Horne and her wonderful team at Authors and Co – So much patience.

Charlie Neary for her amazing copywriting skills and helping to get down on paper all I wanted to say. I couldn't have done it without you.

Lindsey Fairhurst for working alongside me on the course and building the Seed to Vase book club.

Lisa Johnson for guiding me in how to run courses online – I will be forever grateful to you.

And of course, above everything all the participants who gave up their time freely to enable me to write this collection of stories – I am eternally grateful.

And authors everywhere. I have a new found respect for all of you – its an amazing thing to do but I will never under estimate the work involved every again. What a journey and one I have loved.

Lightning Source UK Ltd.
Milton Keynes UK
UKHW020626260122
397727UK00010B/378/J